# FROM SELF-NEGLECT TO SELF-COMPASSION

*A compassionate guide to creating a thriving life*

## DR HAYLEY D QUINN

First published in 2026
Copyright © Dr Hayley D Quinn 2026

All rights reserved. No part of this book may be reproduced or transmitted in any form or by any means, electronic or mechanical, including AI-generated reproductions, photocopying, recording, or by any information storage and retrieval system, without prior written permission from the publisher. The Australian *Copyright Act 1968* (the Act) allows a maximum of one chapter or 10 per cent of this book, whichever is the greater, to be photocopied by any educational institution for its educational purposes provided that the educational institution (or body that administers it) has given a remuneration notice to the Copyright Agency (Australia) under the Act.

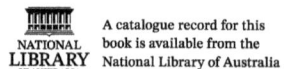

A catalogue record for this book is available from the National Library of Australia

ISBN 978-1-7642074-0-9 paperback
ISBN 978-1-7642074-1-6 eBook

Cover design and illustrations by Gráinne Schäfer
Author photos by Eyes of Love Photography
Typeset in Greycliff CF by Post Pre-press Group, Brisbane

The information in this book is provided for general education and guidance on the topics discussed. It is not intended as, and should not be relied upon as, a substitute for medical, psychological, psychiatric or other professional advice. Readers should seek independent, qualified advice that takes account of their own circumstances. While care has been taken in preparing this material, the author and publisher make no representation or warranty as to its accuracy or completeness and accept no responsibility or liability for any loss, damage or injury that may arise from its use or interpretation.

The Kind Press acknowledges the Traditional Custodians of the land on which we work. We pay respect to Elders past and present and recognise that sovereignty was never ceded. This was and always will be Aboriginal land.

*From Self-Neglect to Self-Compassion* takes you on a journey of self-discovery and self-reflection. Hayley is passionate about burnout prevention and courageously and honestly offers insights into her own personal journey. This book is a valuable resource for individuals seeking to realign with their core values and enhance their overall wellbeing. Through engaging exercises and reflective prompts, this guide empowers you to cultivate self-compassion, whilst also enhancing compassion for others.

—**Dr Elaine Beaumont,** Psychotherapist, Lecturer in Counselling and Psychotherapy at the University of Salford, and Author of The Kindness Workbook, The Compassionate Mind Workbook and The Self-Compassion App

Every person would benefit from having this book in their life! *From Self-Neglect to Self-Compassion* is the roadmap so many ambitious people are missing, one that bridges achievement with genuine wellbeing. Dr Hayley D Quinn offers a gentle yet powerful guide for anyone who has spent too long putting their own needs last, blending structure, evidence and compassion in a way that fits real life. What stands out most is the tone. You feel seen, not judged. Grounded in science and personal insight, Dr Hayley shows that self-compassion is not indulgent or innate, but a skill that can be trained, practised and strengthened over time. This is a warm, wise and practical companion for anyone ready to move from survival to a more aligned and sustainable way of living. You will grow as a result of this book!

—**Jessica Spendlove,** BSc (Nutr), MNurtDiet, Performance Dietician, Executive Health Coach & Wellbeing Speaker

If you are a woman who is hard on herself, always puts others first, and wants more out of life, this book is for you. Dr Quinn offers wise and gentle guidance for living life with greater purpose and self-compassion, while teaching readers to rest, set boundaries, and recharge. I highly recommend this book for any woman with a loud inner critic, teetering on the edge of burnout.

—**Jill Stoddard,** PhD – Author of The Big Book of ACT Metaphors, Be Mighty, and Imposter No More and co-host of the top-ranked podcast, Psychologists Off the Clock

Do you have that one friend who doesn't let you get away with saying, 'I'm fine'? The one who gently sits you down with a cup of tea and says, 'I really want to know all about you'? That's what this beautiful and deeply knowledgeable book from Dr. Hayley Quinn feels like, as her expert voice invites you to trade the exhaustion of self-neglect for the quiet power of self-compassion. This book is a gentle but direct path to understanding why you've been putting yourself last and how to finally and lovingly become your own dearest friend. This deeply empathetic guide is a must-read that has earned a spot at the top of my recommended resources – I know so many of the clients I serve will find solace in Dr Quinn's warm guidance as they rest, heal, and begin to thrive.

—**Tiffany Rochester** – Clinical Psychologist, Founder of Co-Parenting Companion, Past President of ANZ ACBS

This isn't a book, it's the warmest of hugs. After only a few chapters, you would not be at all surprised to look up and find yourself on the comfiest couch, with a cuppa that you didn't make, in your favourite mug. By your side, is the kind of friend who listens, but also tells you what you need to hear (in the gentlest, judgment-free way). Hayley allows you to be yourself but also to see yourself clearly, both now and the self that is still to come. She helps us to recognise the ways that, in seeking to help others, we often harm our most precious resource: ourselves. Instead, we are guided to develop our self-awareness and with that, our capacity to show compassion to ourselves. Neurodiversity is mentioned throughout the book, reminding us that all brains can be tricky, while encouraging us to reflect on what it is that constitutes self-compassion for our unique minds.

—**Adelle Sushames** – Founder Neurodivergent Ally, AuDHD clinical psychologist, speaker, author, and creator of the much-loved ND me, Spoon Thieves, and Spoon Savers cards.

I absolutely loved this book. The way it weaves together lived experience and professional wisdom feels so genuine and deeply human. It creates a beautiful, accessible pathway to self-care that celebrates diversity in every sense and reminds us that there's no one "right" way to move towards healing. Each activity gently guides you back to yourself, inviting reflection and kindness without a trace of judgement. It's thoughtful, compassionate, and quietly powerful.

—**Stacey Vervoort** – Psychologist

Reading Dr Hayley's book is like a warm hug from a friend. Her ability to condense big concepts into bite sized actionable steps is extraordinary. This book is essential reading for anyone who has struggled to befriend their mind.

—**Amy Campbell** – Clinical Psychologist & Sex Educator, Author of The Mindful Sex Guide.

Reading Dr Hayley Quinn's beautiful, practical and thought-provoking work, *From Self-Neglect to Self-Compassion*, feels like talking to a wise and caring friend. A friend who understands the exhaustion of constantly saying "yes" to everyone except yourself. A friend who gently guides you back to what matters. One of the book's greatest strengths is how it translates complex psychological theory into vivid, relatable insights. Dr Hayley's writing style mirrors her message. It is intelligent, wise, and deeply caring. Step by step, she leads us through how to understand and cultivate compassion in our lives, so that we can thrive, and those around us can too. *From Self-Neglect to Self-Compassion* reads like a love letter to those of us who have forgotten that our needs matter. It's a book to linger over, to return to when the world grows loud, and to share with others who are ready to make changes too. Dr Hayley reminds us throughout, "Go gently with yourself," and she helps us to do just that. Right now, in a society that demands that we constantly prove our worth, choosing gentleness and compassion might be the bravest thing we can do.

—**Emily Wilkinson** – Clinical Psychologist, award-winning poet, facilitator, and coach. Founder of Flourishing Space

Dr Hayley D. Quinn's *From Self-Neglect to Self-Compassion* is a refreshingly real, intelligent, and deeply human guide for change. Grounded in psychology and self-efficacy, Hayley offers practical, compassionate tools that empower readers, particularly neurodivergent women, to create lives that feel authentic and sustainable. She writes without fluff or false promises, blending insight with humility, warmth, and gentle humour. This book dismantles self-criticism and perfectionism with evidence-based compassion and genuine care. Hayley reminds us that change begins with honesty, courage, and the willingness to choose ourselves, one small act at a time.

—**Indiana Holley** – Editor-in-Chief & Founder, Creating the Muse

Reading *From Self-Neglect to Self-Compassion* felt like being gently held by someone who understands the very particular ache of women who've spent years giving more than they had to give. Dr Hayley Quinn writes with such clarity, kindness and truth. This isn't another self-help book that tells you to 'do more' – it's a guide that shows you how to finally *be with yourself* in a way that's nourishing, sustainable and real. As a neurodivergent woman, mother, and business leader, I genuinely recognised myself on almost every page. Hayley's blend of lived experience and professional wisdom makes this a life-changing read for anyone who's ever felt guilty for needing rest, or who is unsure how to show up for themselves without letting others down. I finished this book feeling seen, steadied, and reminded that compassion – not perfection – is the most powerful leadership tool we have.

—**Cherie Clonan** – proudly Autistic CEO at The Digital Picnic

This might be one of the most important books you'll read as a seasoned professional. Hayley's book might not be for those just starting out in a career; that's when we're full of vim and vigor. Yet when we are so busy we start putting others first, neglecting ourselves, prepping the ground for burnt out. I'm grateful Hayley has been so revealing with us about how to transform those patterns to flourish.

—**Deirdre Fay,** MSW – Author of Becoming Safely Embodied(2021), Attachment-Based Yoga & Meditation for Trauma Recovery(2017), co-author of Attachment Disturbances in Adults (2016) and co-author of chapters in Neurobiological Treatments of Traumatic Dissociation

This book is dedicated to my darling, Matt

You are the greatest gift I have ever received. Your presence has made me value my presence here all the more and allowed me to see myself through a different lens. May life offer you many amazing opportunities as it has me. Always remember to walk your own path, darling, and choose the life that your heart calls for.
I love you so dearly.

# Contents

Who this book is for     xi
Introduction     xiii
A Bit About Me     xix

## PART I: START WHERE YOU ARE
1  Getting to Know Yourself     3
2  Caring for All of You     23
3  Making Sense of Feelings and the Beliefs that Hold You Back     57

## PART II: EXPLORE THE POSSIBILITIES
4  What Happened to Your Dreams?     79
5  What Matters Most to You?     86
6  Connecting to the Wisdom of Your Future Self     94

## PART III: LEARN TO DO IT DIFFERENTLY; CHOOSE YOU
7  Permission to Put Yourself First     115

| 8 | The Courage to Choose Compassion | 129 |
| 9 | Time to Prioritise You | 153 |

**PART IV: FINDING YOUR NEW WAY OF BEING**

| 10 | The Parts of Life That Need Your Care | 205 |
| 11 | Coming Home to Your Compassionate Self | 223 |
| 12 | Go Gently with Yourself | 232 |

| Recommended Reading | 241 |
| Acknowledgements | 243 |
| References | 248 |
| About the author | 251 |
| Where to from here | 253 |

# Who this book is for

*For every woman who has ever longed for time for herself.*

*For every woman who has listened to the
cruelty of her own inner voice.*

*For every woman who has always put others' needs before hers.*

*For every woman who has dreamt about
a life that feels like a good fit.*

*For every woman who has ever felt like she deserves more from life.*

*For every woman who knows things need
to change but feels stuck.*

# *Introduction*

Welcome, it is so lovely that you're here and taking time to care about you and a life that feels aligned. One that you can feel excited about.

There are many books out there designed to make you a better version of yourself. Now, while they may well help you become a better version of yourself, I suspect you are already pretty damn amazing, but you just don't let yourself acknowledge that. That is why this book is a bit different. Within these pages, you will feel seen, understood and supported. I'm not here to make you better. I'm here to help you get to know yourself better, to shine a light on how you might be neglecting yourself, and to show you that life can be better.

This book has been designed in such a way that you can read a chapter or two and still feel like you have completed something you came here to do. It is designed to be informative, soothing, reflective, nurturing and ultimately life changing. I've walked this path and my life changed significantly for the better, so I do know it's possible.

## FROM SELF-NEGLECT TO SELF-COMPASSION

This isn't about adding to the burden of everything you're already managing. This book is about you, the relationship you have with yourself, your wellbeing and the life you desire. In some parts, it may challenge you to think about yourself in ways you previously haven't. I hope it does, because those challenges and discomforts are the reasons we choose to make change.

This book will help you to bring compassion into your life so you can utilise your own wisdom, and care for yourself in the way that you so beautifully care for others. With compassion as your companion, I believe you can create a life that fits more fully with who you are and how you want your life to be. I also believe that in bringing compassion to yourself, you will enhance and maintain your capacity for caring for others. This can allow you to keep caring for others in your family, community and the world as a whole, whilst also holding yourself in mind as you live a life that feels meaningful and suits who you are.

As you read this book, you may notice that you want to make some different choices in your life, work or relationships and I trust this will add to your strength, courage and wisdom to change what doesn't work for you and to start living your life differently.

There isn't one path or one right way to be in the world. We each need to find our own way that is right for us. I certainly will not claim to be an expert on your life. Only you know how you truly think, feel and behave. I will however share with you my knowledge, wisdom and learnings. This is not a prescription for how you should live your life, or how to engage in your relationships or work. Instead, it is a gentle invitation to reflect on yourself, your needs and your wellbeing, and most of all, how you can best take care of yourself so you can live the life you desire.

# INTRODUCTION

*'My mission in life is not merely to survive, but to thrive; and to do so with some passion, some compassion, some humour, and some style.'* —MAYA ANGELOU

So many women I talk to and work with are going through life simply surviving or compromising on what they want. Settling for a smaller, diluted, less colourful life than they desire. It breaks my heart because I know the pain and numbness of living that way. I don't want that for anyone. I want to help you live your life on whatever volume you want. I want to help you come home to yourself, embrace who you are, confidently use your voice, take up space and live the life you desire. Let's disrupt some of the unhelpful and toxic narratives that we have been shadowed by for too long.

This book is not intended to minimise the impact of systemic problems. These issues are real, and they matter. While this book focuses on what we can change in our own lives right now, it does so with the understanding that individual change does not replace the need for broader social change. It is a guide to help you make changes in your life that may flow into your family, your community, and if you feel able, contribute to change in the wider systems we live within. I acknowledge the many barriers and restrictions placed on women around the world and in no way mean to minimise the suffering and oppression of these women. I acknowledge my own privilege in being able to make choices that I know many women cannot yet make.

I have met many women across my life. Some have self-loathing as their default, some embrace and love themselves, and some feel engaged and immersed in a life they love that feels meaningful, aligned and satisfying. Their life holds space for them as the unique human being that they are. Some women move through life feeling 'fine' in their relationships and how they see themselves. They aren't plagued by too much self-doubt and self-criticism, but they also aren't fully immersed in a life that allows them to expand and evolve. It's as if there is a magical element that they haven't yet discovered but that they know something is out there for them.

Wherever you are in your life, no matter what your internal dialogue sounds like or how your external life looks, whether you already have a regular self-care practice, and self-compassion is a familiar concept, or self-care and self-compassion are new to you, this book is for you.

> The terms 'woman' and 'women' are used throughout this book for ease of reading. They are intended to include anyone who identifies as a woman, non-binary, or gender diverse with full respect for all gender identities.
>
> The term 'work' is used in this book to refer to paid employment. This is not intended to overlook or diminish the value of unpaid work, which plays a vital role in most households and communities.

I will share with you stories of mine and those of other women I have had the pleasure of talking with, stories that I believe will help you feel seen, may offer a validation of sorts to your lived experience and inspire and give you hope that life can be different. The process of changing my relationship with myself has been profound and truly life-changing. I know that access to this process isn't the same for everyone and that our circumstances, systems, resources and histories all play a part. But I also believe that no matter where you

## INTRODUCTION

come from, who you are, or whether you believe you deserve a better life, some form of change is possible, even in small ways, for all of us.

For meaningful change to happen, we need to engage in different ways of thinking and doing. It's not enough to read a book or take a course and hope that the learnings along with some magic will miraculously appear and change everything. This is why throughout the following pages, I invite you to pause, to inhale and exhale gently and to reflect on thoughtful questions and engage in guided meditations. I encourage you to take your time and only engage to the level that feels right for you in any given moment. Be aware of what arises and go gently with yourself. Remember, you can always come back to a particular question or meditation when you are ready. I will say, do your best to not let that be your default process. If you notice you are avoiding anything, be curious and ask if this is a familiar pattern of avoidance. If instead you don't feel resourced enough to do it in that moment, return as soon as you are ready. This is a time to be radically honest with yourself. It doesn't matter to anyone else if you do these. It does matter to you and your future self.

You will want to take notes throughout, so do this in whatever form works best for you. This might be a pen and paper journal, electronic notetaking, voice recordings or having someone assist you to make notes.

I thank you for being here, because when we take care of ourselves and bring compassion into our lives, the more we can create a world that is compassionate, fair, accepting and peaceful for everyone. Now, it's time to focus on your Self.

Go well and go gently with yourself,
Dr Hayley

*Caring for yourself is not an item to tick off your to-do list. It is an ongoing lifelong process of being aware of yourself, turning towards, checking in, reflecting and taking compassionate action.*

# *A Bit About Me*

I was born in the UK, to parents of different cultures. My mum had moved there as a young adult where she met and married my dad, a marriage that lasted until I was seventeen years old. We didn't speak my mum's native language, but we did follow some of her traditions. Whilst the differing cultures weren't really discussed, I have no doubt they played a part in shaping how I saw the world. I was the younger of two children and grew up in a small village in the northwest of England. I played in the street until dark with the neighbourhood kids, which I mostly enjoyed, but what I really loved was escaping into a good book or making mud pies, rose petal perfume and dolls out of the cardboard tubes inside toilet rolls.

I struggled with self-doubt and self-hatred throughout my childhood and well into adulthood. I often had the feeling that I'd been dropped off on the wrong planet, or that I was trying to navigate a game without knowing the rules. By the time I was fifteen, after years of struggling with my mental health, I thought the only solution was to no longer be here. I'll never forget the sense of loneliness and hopelessness I felt sitting on my bed with pills in hand on that day I chose as my last. I am now so thankful that things didn't go the way I had planned, though at the time, it just felt like one more thing I had failed at. My heart breaks for that younger part of me. I sometimes imagine my present self sitting beside her, giving her a loving hug and telling her how gorgeous she is, how wonderful her life will be and how happy I am that she stayed.

By the time I had decided to leave school, which was earlier than many of my peers, I had got to the point where I didn't turn up to sit some of my exams and I spent a lot of my school days playing truant. My academic achievement was pretty dismal and for years I labelled myself as a school dropout, not something I would call someone else. For decades, I carried the belief that I was stupid and wouldn't achieve much in my life. That I would be stuck in unfulfilling jobs and that was my fault. I now know, amongst other struggles, I was trying to fit myself into a system that wasn't built for my type of brain.

My personal life wasn't much better. I treated myself in ways that diminished and disrespected who I was. I struggled to recognise warning signs in relationships, and I tolerated behaviours from others that I didn't deserve nor would tolerate today. At twenty-five, I decided to leave England and travel to Australia via Hong Kong. Many people told me it was a brave move. I recognise that now, but at the time I didn't feel brave. I just knew somewhere inside me that it was necessary. It seemed like a good way to change how I was living and try something else. So, I set off on my backpacking adventure and made a commitment to myself that I was going to try new things and also figure out who I was and what I wanted for myself. I took my sweet time doing that and made plenty of mistakes along the way which served to strengthen my self-critic. I mean, that sneaky little critic doesn't miss an opportunity, right?

## A BIT ABOUT ME

My backpacking was meant to be for a year, but life had different plans, as it sometimes does. I stayed permanently in Australia and settled in the beautiful river city of Meanjin (Brisbane), a stark contrast to the cold, wet and grey of northern England. At age twenty-nine, my precious baby boy was born. I couldn't believe how much joy I felt, and yet the happiest time of my life was overshadowed by domestic violence. Within a year, I chose safety. With my son just an infant, I continued life as a single parent. I felt scared and uncertain about the future but knew without a doubt this was the best choice for the wellbeing of me and my darling boy. If I'm honest, it was my son's safety and wellbeing that motivated me back then, rather than my own. A large part of me thought the relationship I had was what I deserved.

Over the years, I continued to make mistakes. I also started to make choices to change how I felt about myself and my life. I challenged the beliefs I had about my capabilities and what I deserved, and I allowed myself to take risks that both scared and excited me. I went to university to study psychology, the whole time feeling like an imposter. I was one of the oldest students sitting in class, I was recovering from a traumatic relationship and I was a 'school dropout'. Surely, I didn't really belong. But I kept learning, passing exams and getting high grades and to my utmost surprise, received an academic achievement award each year. I spent nine years at university completing a Bachelor of Psychology, Honours and a Clinical PhD. I was fascinated by what I was learning, felt accomplished when I got good grades and made beautiful friends, some of whom are my most cherished friends to this day. I lived on government assistance and casual pay, and at times, worked up to three jobs to provide for us. I also had long university holidays which allowed me to spend school holidays with my son. Looking back, this is something I am so very grateful for. These were the hardest and most wonderful years of my life to that point.

During the final stages of my PhD, I met my husband, a caring, gentle, kind, funny and compassionate man, and one of my greatest supporters. I embarked on my career as a psychologist and soon made the choice to work for myself. I loved my clients and felt privileged to hear their stories. From the outside, my life looked wonderful. I had a PhD, a thriving practice, a wonderful husband and son, and a home I loved. But beneath it all, I was unravelling, feeling scared, uncertain and desperately unwell. I was passionate about helping others, but I wasn't stopping to consider my own needs. Squeezing in extra appointments and spending long days listening to stories filled with loss, grief and trauma was taking its toll on me. I kept ignoring the warning signs, the headaches, fatigue, brain fog, increased anxiety and self-doubt. My self-critic was so strong and ever-present. My inner voice kept telling me to keep pushing through. I compared myself to others and wondered why I wasn't coping. What was wrong with me? Eventually, I had no choice. I had to pay attention. I was severely burnt out. Everyday tasks became overwhelming. Some days I couldn't get off the couch. I struggled to recognise the woman I had become. Reaching that low point was devastating. I had worked so hard to achieve my degrees and build up my practice, and I didn't know if I would be able to continue working as a psychologist, or at all. On reflection, it's no surprise I was burnt out. I was trying to do too much, for too long and not taking adequate care of myself.

As difficult as this time was, it also became a turning point that put me on a path to thriving. I began to change how I related to myself and offered myself the same compassion I so easily extend to others. My training in Compassion Focused Therapy helped

## A BIT ABOUT ME

me to understand the impacts of how I'd been living, and, in that process, I discovered a new way of being with myself. One where I no longer had to earn my worth through achievement or overwork, but could instead embrace who I am and live in a way that suits me, in alignment with my values and caring for myself as much as I care for others. As my health and confidence returned, my life expanded again. My days of barely being able to get off the couch changed to travelling overseas to present in places like New York, Singapore and Edinburgh. I went from struggling to make it through the day to creating a life and business that feels authentic and sustainable. When I was identified as Autistic with ADHD at age fifty-two, a lot of my past started to make more sense. Following my identification as neurodivergent, I continued to make changes to my life and work, including an intentional choice to leave the psychology profession after almost two decades. My business evolved in another direction, and I now travel, speak, and coach others, sharing the message I needed to hear myself: you don't have to sacrifice your wellbeing to make a difference. In fact, when you thrive, your life and work will too.

I had no idea the choices I'd make would lead me to a life that now feels so beautiful, meaningful, connected, aligned and worthwhile. My life so far has taken me on a journey from wondering whether life was worth living, to changing the relationship with myself and living a life full of wonder, embracing life with curiosity, passion and compassion.

But this book isn't about me. It's about you and the life you want to create. So, I invite you to come on a journey with me.

*To really know yourself, you need to
allow stillness and have a willingness
to be open to your experiences.*

*This can be challenging and at times painful.
You won't always like what you see. If you can
offer compassion to yourself for your suffering,
and acknowledge you are part of a human
family that suffers and struggles with the tricky
brain you have been born with, you can move
towards a place of choice and growth.*

*Slow it down ... breathe ... go within ...*

*Welcome to Self®*

PART I

# START WHERE YOU ARE

# 1

# *Getting to Know Yourself*

You are a beautiful, unique, complex and interesting human being. Yes, you. Even if you don't believe that yet, I absolutely know it to be true.

You have complexities and characteristics that influence how you navigate the world, and the world has so many different aspects that influence you. You have facets about you that you may not see for yourself and yet others may see quite clearly. You have relationships with others, and you have a relationship with yourself, whether you pay attention to that or not. A good relationship takes time and effort to cultivate. Like any relationship, the one you have with yourself doesn't just happen. It requires of you your time, attention, curiosity and willingness. If you are open to these, you gift yourself the opportunity to not only change the relationship you have with yourself but also to change your life and your relationship with others. Whilst it takes effort and willingness to do things differently, in my experience, it is so worth it!

## FROM SELF-NEGLECT TO SELF-COMPASSION

*The longest, closest and most significant relationship you will ever have is the one you have with yourself.*

So many people stay disconnected and distant from themselves. I get it. That's how I used to walk through the world. Being in touch with myself felt too painful, but being detached from myself led me to living a life that was filled with pain, even if I tried to ignore it. A life that was, for the most part, lacking joy, fulfilment and respect for myself and any dreams I had, if I even allowed myself to dream.

For me, one aspect of this relationship-building with myself has been a practice of asking myself questions the way I would if I met someone new and wanted to get to know them better. Asking myself questions and then listening to the answers and learning to respond in the best way I can. Of course, I don't always do this well. I still have times when I forget about me in the process of something else, but now I know I can come back to myself and check back in anytime. I am an ongoing work of art, and no doubt always will be. We all are.

The key is getting to know yourself.

As humans, we're always in context with something or someone. You are a child to parents; you are a partner, lover, spouse to the other in a relationship; you are a parent to your child; you are a business owner because you operate a business; you are a paid employee in your workplace; you are an artist because there is art you created; you are an author of the book that exists because you wrote it. See where I'm going with this?

I invite you to think about yourself for a moment, and if there are any thoughts, feelings or discomfort that show up, just be curious. Just try to hold it lightly. Often our distress or discomfort comes from the meaning we attach to our thoughts and feelings rather than the thoughts and feelings themselves. So as best you can, just notice what your experience is rather than trying to analyse it or make sense of it. Tricky for a human mind, I know. We will cover more about your tricky mind very soon.

You can think about yourself in terms of who you are personally, who you are within your family, community, culture and environment. You can consider what spirituality or religion means to you or what gender means to you. You can explore and be curious about your neurotype. You may already identify as either neurodivergent[1] or neurotypical. Many women I speak to and work with find themselves questioning who they are and why certain things have felt so different or difficult for them, and then go on to discover they are neurodivergent. This seems to happen for many women approaching perimenopause and in their menopause era. If you are questioning your neurotype, it's encouraging to know that there are now many resources available. I know for me, understanding my neurodivergent identity has been really helpful in understanding my strengths and challenges and has increased my level of self-compassion.

It's important to know yourself to really understand what does and doesn't work for you, to know what replenishes your energy and what depletes you, and to uncover the things you enjoy and those that you find more stressful or just not enjoyable. Understanding who you are allows you to appreciate how you like to engage with the world. It helps you recognise your capacities and capabilities. You can then think about how you want your life to be, how you would like your business to be, or how you would like to navigate the different roles you occupy, whether these are personal, work-related

---

1   Neurodivergent refers to people whose brains function atypically and includes, but is not limited to, autism, ADHD, dyslexia, dyscalculia, dyspraxia

or any other role in your life. Keep in mind that some of these roles will likely be for a number of years. Therefore, you want to make sure they are sustainable. When we are clearer on who we are and how we can best move through the world, it can be easier to design our life in alignment with what will help us thrive.

## *Pause*

I invite you to take a moment and consider how you see yourself. Think about all your relationships, different roles, likes, dislikes, strengths and challenges. Then answer the question below. There are no right or wrong responses. Just be curious about what comes up.

*When I think about myself, who am I?*

Now, can you see how you are more than one-dimensional, and can you see more of the complexity of who you really are? You're a kaleidoscope of fascinating qualities, experiences and connections, deserving a life that fits with who you are and how you want to live. This may be a radical idea for those of us who have felt like we have to be a certain way to fit in, or have been told we have to be a certain way to achieve the things we want.

To create an aligned life, I believe there are two key factors:

1) Knowing yourself
2) Compassion

Let's begin with some information that will help you know yourself better. We're going to start broad, and as we move through the book together, we will focus in on you as the unique human being you are. It's one thing to understand ourselves as part of the human race and quite another layer entirely to understand our own unique ways of being. It's the combination of this understanding when partnered with compassion in our lives that gives us the roadmap and allows us to learn the skills we need to truly thrive.

## What it means to be a human with a tricky brain

Before we start to explore what it means to live, work and relate to ourselves and others in ways that feel more aligned and sustainable, we need to start with understanding our humanness and how our mind works.

My personal and professional life has been influenced in the most positive and profound ways by Compassion Focused Therapy (CFT), a psychological approach developed by Professor Paul Gilbert OBE. Originally created to support people experiencing intense emotional pain, shame and self-criticism, the wisdom found in CFT is relevant to all of us. CFT helps us see that we are not broken; we're just humans with tricky brains, shaped by evolution and our experiences. These brains are doing their best to keep us safe, even when their strategies (like self-criticism, overthinking, or shutdown) feel anything but helpful. When we can understand ourselves with compassion, everything begins to shift. We can stop blaming ourselves for feeling overwhelmed, reactive or 'not enough'. We can start to change the relationship we have with ourselves to one that is gentle, kinder and more supportive. A relationship that sets the foundation for all aspects of our life.

## FROM SELF-NEGLECT TO SELF-COMPASSION

We were born with a brain that we did not design. I'm sure if we had a choice, the brain we'd choose wouldn't get so easily caught up in worry, rumination (repetitive and negative thinking), social comparison, self-doubt, catastrophising (worst-case scenario) and all those other tricky mental gymnastics that ours does.

Our brain is designed to respond to threats, with an inbuilt 'better safe than sorry system' that is always on alert. It is a system that helped our ancestors survive, and it's the reason we are here. A problem we have in today's modern society is that we are bombarded with messages that activate our threat system all too easily.

Think about the number of times you compare yourself to someone else. Maybe they look more successful, or have something you wish you had. Think about the number of times your brain tells you that you've still got what feels like a million tasks to get through. Then there are the 'not good enough' – friend, partner, parent, business owner, employee, feel free to add yours here – thoughts. Your mind can also wander off easily, and often at the most inopportune times. You can be mid-sentence and before you know it, you're thinking about something completely unrelated to your conversation. Please tell me that's not just me and my ADHD brain. Have you ever been in the middle of doing something only to find yourself thinking about something that happened last week? Yep, your tricky brain will do that. It's not your fault.

Your brain is designed to warn you about any and all dangers. If you're chatting with someone who mentions something challenging that is similar to your history, it may bring up a memory which could be in the form of an image, thought, feeling or physical sensation. At the time, you may or may not recognise what it is; you just feel a discomfort. If, in those moments, you're unable to acknowledge your humanness and what arises, then how can you take care of yourself in a way that will be long-lasting, effective and sustainable? Now, I'm not saying you stop mid-conversation and start focusing only on you; that probably won't serve you too well in your relationships. What I am saying is you'll benefit from noticing what happened, holding it lightly whilst in conversation and then taking care of how you feel later. Don't ignore your suffering. Don't lose sight of yourself.

When you have numerous demanding and competing roles, you have to find ways to sustain yourself. We know that caring responsibilities, whether for children, households or ageing parents or relatives, still often fall more heavily on women and gender-diverse people, even when they're also working full time. This is true across many types of families, including same-sex and blended relationships. Please do not forget that while you move through these roles, you are not here only to serve others, no matter how strongly you have received that message throughout your life. You're a human being who has a variety of emotions, and you have a history that impacts how you respond to people, stories and events. You're a human with a tricky mind, just like your friends, family members, colleagues and every other human being on the planet.

You engage in different roles with different people at different times throughout your life. You may be working with others, supporting them to take better care of themselves; you might be working hard in your business or career to support your family with what they need; or you might be in a season of managing your family relationships and household tasks. During these times, I have no doubt you do your best to offer the best of you, even if you don't think your best is good enough. You want others to be happy and taken care of. Many of us were given a doll with a nappy, bottle and a pile of clothes when we were little, or maybe a toy kitchen with pots and pans and little plastic food items and encouraged through play, intentionally or not, to learn how to care for others. It makes sense that your mind is other-focused.

We have a societal narrative that says, 'You're meant to care for others. You're okay, you know how to manage all of this. You are Superwoman.' But what if we don't know how to manage it all? What if we are not okay and don't feel like we can manage? What if other aspects of our life are making it hard to sit in the roles of partner, parent, business owner, employee and caregiver? What then?

What if by allowing yourself some time to process how you feel, things could be different? By slowing down and turning inwards, you can listen to the parts of yourself that are suffering. You can acknowledge what is happening, and if you are willing to tolerate the discomfort that shows up in those times, you will be more able to tend to your needs in a helpful way. Imagine what it might be like if you treated yourself, in those moments, the same way you treat someone you love and care deeply for.

## *Pause*

Take a moment to reflect on the questions below. Write down any thoughts and feelings that show up for you.

- *How often do I stop to consider how I will take care of myself?*
- *What would it look like if I took care of myself the way I take care of others?*
- *Do I think it is okay to think about myself in this way?*

> - *What might be some consequences of not taking care of myself? (Maybe you're already experiencing some of them.)*

It can be helpful to remember that everything in life is interconnected. We don't just go to work, or anywhere, and forget about everything else that is going on. We don't stop loving family, or caring about friends, or feeling concerned about our current personal problems, or grieving our losses, just because we're in our workspace. Similarly, we don't automatically stop thinking about work because the clock says it's the end of our workday.

For example, if you've had a stressful day, that might lead to an evening where you feel disgruntled, distressed, angry, ashamed or inadequate. This can have negative impacts, not only on your wellbeing but on your relationships too. If you don't take care of the parts of you that are feeling this distress, it leaves you open to further distress and the risk of spiralling into a negative mindset that can colour the rest of your evening. It can lead to you being distant or irritated with the people close to you, causing ruptures in your close relationships which can then lead to a feeling of instability and further distress, preventing you from seeking the support that would be helpful. It's not hard to see how this can keep compounding itself.

## *Pause*

Take a moment to think about the following questions. You can write down your thoughts if that feels helpful, or sit and reflect on your answers.

- *How is your home life impacted when your day hasn't gone as you would have liked?*
- *How are you with yourself?*
- *How are you with the people close to you?*

This isn't an exercise in shaming yourself if you've realised that you behave in ways you would rather you didn't. It is an opportunity to understand yourself better and to recognise that life can be hard.

> 'The core of who I am threads through all of my life: the woman who wants a full and meaningful life; the mother who wonders how her adult son is going and when they might next get together; the wife who values her loving husband and wonders if getting busier with work will somehow negatively impact the stability of that union; the daughter who wonders when she will next venture overseas and see her elderly parents.
>
> I cannot remove the human that is me from any of these roles and nor would I want to. My humanness, my willingness to be real, raw and vulnerable in all of my roles is what brings them to life. My humanness in my business is, I believe, one of my greatest assets and makes me the warm, caring, compassionate, and attuned person that I am. It also means I feel deeply and that can be taxing, and I need to be very aware of myself and my

> own needs as I navigate my days. I need to practise what I teach and draw on the learning I have; to not only take care of those around me but also myself.'

## The Three Circle Model

CFT gives us a powerful framework to understand our emotion regulation system using the three-circle model which outlines our threat, drive and soothing system. In a society that is obsessed with us doing more and more, it can be helpful to recognise when we are motivated by fear or achievement, as well as how we can connect to ourselves in a way that feels calm and grounded. This isn't just good for our nervous system but essential to our long-term wellbeing. If we stay stuck between threat and drive, we can develop an imbalance that can lead us into burnout, even when we are engaging in things we love.

If you're someone who likes to take a deeper dive with your understanding, there's certainly lots of information available. I've added some reading recommendations in the resources section at the end of this book. For now, let's go with the brief, easy-to-digest version. Believe me, it's a game-changer.

Each of the three emotional systems are important. They operate in different ways, depending on our motivation, and they each have their own set of thoughts, feelings and behaviours.

### Threat system (red circle)

This is your 'better safe than sorry' system. It's on twenty-four hours a day, seven days a week. The threat system's primary role is to keep you safe. It's about protection and seeking safety so that if you find yourself under threat, your body will naturally prepare you for a fight/flight/freeze/fawn response. These are the escape and attack responses you are biologically wired to experience. For many people, this system is highly sensitive, particularly if there's trauma in your history. The following analogy might help explain this.

When you put an alarm on a car, it's designed to activate and sound the alarm when someone breaks into the car – when there is an actual threat. Some car alarms are highly sensitive, though. You know the ones. They go off in your street when a cat jumps on the bonnet or if it's a particularly windy day. No real threat, but the alarm activates anyway. This is how some people's threat systems operate. There only needs to be something that could seem like a threat and there they are in that fight/flight/freeze/fawn response.

When your threat system (red circle) is dominant, your thoughts will be narrower in focus, based around the threat, and you're more likely to ruminate over past events, catastrophise about outcomes and be hyper-vigilant. You might be avoidant, submissive, dissociative or aggressive and the feelings you experience when you're in your threat system include anxiety, fear, anger and disgust. You might experience a higher heart rate, dry mouth, an upset stomach and tension in your body.

### Drive system (blue circle)

This system motivates you towards the things you desire, want and need. For example, if you're thirsty, you'll be motivated to go and get a drink. When hungry, you'll be motivated to find food. If you're looking to do something new in your business, you'll be motivated towards the things that will help you achieve what you want. I think as women, we can regularly be stuck in drive. There always seems to be a never-ending list of things to do, right! On top of that, for those of us who are neurodivergent, we can get caught up in hyperfocus and sometimes forget to eat and hydrate, or even put off going to the bathroom! To assist with this, I set alarms in my phone to remind me that it's lunchtime, dinnertime, or time for something else I have to do. If I didn't do this, I could sometimes just go all day getting excited about what I'm working on.

When your drive system (blue circle) is dominant, your thoughts will be narrower in focus, based on exploration and seeking out what you desire. You might be restless, more engaged, socialising with others or celebrating. The feelings you experience when you're in your drive system include determination, enthusiasm, wanting and excitement. You might experience a higher heart rate and feel inclined to take action.

### Soothing system (green circle)

This is your 'rest and digest', 'tend and befriend' system. It allows you to rest your body and mind, digest your food and connect to yourself and others in a calm and grounded state. When you're not under threat and you're not trying to pursue anything, you can be in your soothing system. This is the system that helps you rest and restore.

When your soothing system (green circle) is dominant, your thoughts will be more open-minded, reflective and focused on being helpful. You're likely to be kind and friendly, and you'll feel calm, grounded and a sense of safeness and contentment.

Unfortunately for many people, particularly if you have experienced less than ideal caregiving as a child and not had someone to help soothe you when you were little, this system can be underdeveloped.

## THREE CIRCLE MODEL OF EMOTION REGULATION

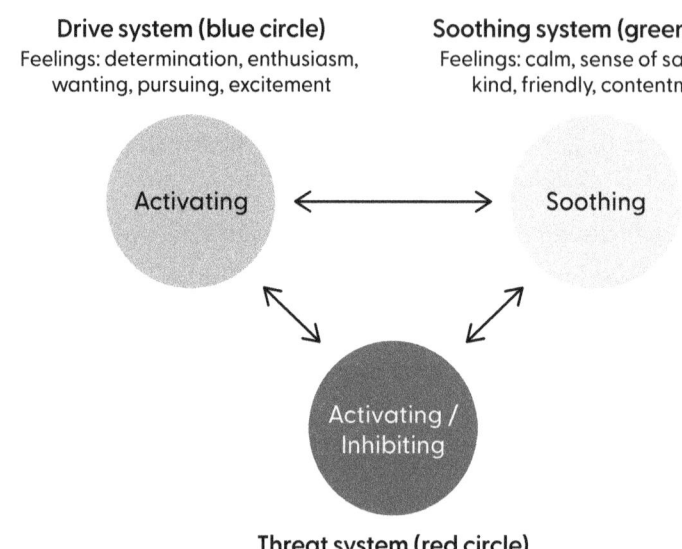

Adapted from Gilbert, The Compassionate Mind (2009), with permission from Little, Brown Book Group.

When your soothing system is underdeveloped or you're not used to accessing this soothing system, you can end up using your drive system to try to regulate when you're feeling stressed (threat system). This is what is often referred to as *threat-based drive*.

For example, something happens to you that makes you feel anxious. Rather than engaging in soothing behaviours, you move into drive and start getting busy. You might do some online shopping, start answering emails, or do work tasks or something else that feels productive. You might reach for food despite not being hungry, or alcohol or other drugs in an attempt to help yourself feel better. There are many ways you can shift into drive to attempt to soothe yourself. Unfortunately, this can keep you stuck in a loop between threat and drive. You attempt to soothe in a way that leads you to feel stress, guilt or shame, and then you find yourself right back in your threat system. When you're in threat-based drive, it's not that the threat system is the only system at play. The three systems are always engaged; they're just out of balance. When you're in threat-based drive, the threat and drive systems are dominant.

You might like to think of the ways this shows up for you. Remember, don't judge yourself. Just be curious. You're doing the best you can with the knowledge, skills and resources you have.

**EXAMPLE OF THREAT-BASED DRIVE**

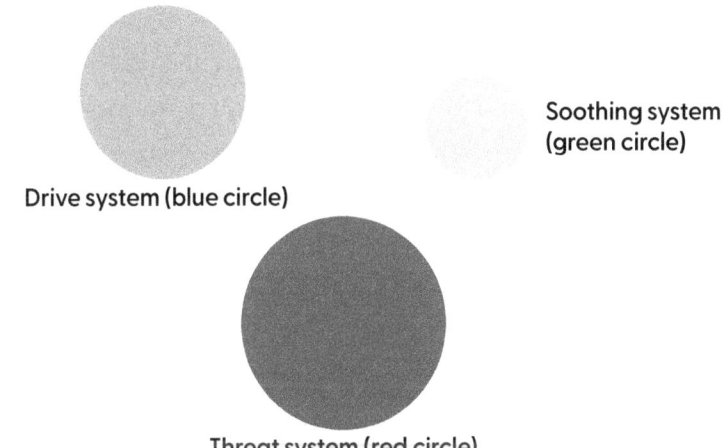

Adapted from Gilbert, The Compassionate Mind (2009), with permission from Little, Brown Book Group.

Ideally, you want your emotional system to be in balance. I say ideally because it is highly unlikely that you're wandering around all day with a perfectly balanced emotional system, so let's drop that expectation right now. I mentioned earlier that each system operates differently, depending on your motivation, those being either competitive or compassionate.

### Competitive motivation

When in an active state of competitive motivation, you might be trying to prove your worth or show that you are somehow 'better than'. You might be trying to prove this to others, or to yourself. Your emotional systems are likely out of balance at this point, and your threat system dominant. When you are motivated by threat, it can feel scary, and you're more likely to be critical and hostile to yourself and others.

### Compassionate motivation

Having a compassionate motivation assists you in connecting with your wisdom, courage and your commitment to be helpful, not harmful, to yourself and others. This helps you bring your emotional systems into balance. When they are more balanced, you can feel calm, connected and capable of making choices that are values-aligned.

I invite you now to think about what your three circles look like in this moment. If you want to, take some time to draw them. Which circle might be the largest, or how imbalanced would those circles be? You can do a quick drawing with a pen, or if you feel like being more creative, you can grab a red, blue and green pencil or crayon. You might find it helpful to draw your circles at a few different times over the next few days to get used to checking in with yourself. If drawing them doesn't appeal to you, just imagine what they would look like. If you're feeling overwhelmed and anxious, your threat system will be the most activated. If you're feeling depressed and unmotivated, your drive system will be decreased. If you're feeling calm and connected, your threat, drive and soothing systems will likely be balanced.

Remember, these three circles will look different at different times throughout your day, so there is no 'right' way to draw these. You can't get this wrong.

## Self-care and the three circles

I find it helpful to consider the three-circle model and pay attention to how my nervous system reacts when I think about ways to take care of myself.

Think about the types of things that trigger a threat response for you. Are there certain self-care activities that trigger a threat response? Do you feel anxious or overwhelmed just thinking about engaging in self-care? Perhaps the idea of caring for yourself brings up thoughts of scarcity, inadequacy or not being good enough, and this leaves you stuck in your threat system. I have been managing a painful shoulder and at times, I have been motivated to exercise in order to take care of myself but have also noticed some threat-system activation because of the fear of making my shoulder worse. In those moments, it's been important for me to bring my emotional system back into balance and connect with my reasons for exercise. It also prompts me to adjust my exercise so I care for my health without causing further injury.

Paying attention to what motivates your engagement in self-care is also important. Remember threat-based drive? We don't want your reasons for self-care to be threat-driven. For example, you might have the thought, 'If I don't take care of myself and I can't work or run my business, I'm not going to make any money, and then I'm going to go broke and I'll be homeless.' On and on the fear thoughts go. This type of thinking activates your nervous system in a way that is unhelpful. So, is it really self-care? There are many ways our threat system motivates our decision-making and impacts our self-care. As someone with a history of disordered eating and obsessive exercise, I am well aware of the threat-based drive that can dress itself up as self-care. So, please be aware of your motivations.

You might take care of yourself because you feel worthwhile, or to look good, or maybe you just think you 'should' take care of yourself. You might want to feel fit enough to play with your children or grandchildren. You might be motivated by a desire to improve or maintain your health. For example, I work with an exercise physiologist. I don't go for fun, although I'll admit we do have some laughs, probably because I don't take myself too seriously. I'm motivated to take care of not just my present self but my future self too. I'll often check in with my eighty-year-old self and ask her what she would want me to do.

Some people are very motivated by the fact that if they look after themselves, they can then look after everybody else, and that's great. I'd hope that it isn't your only motivation. Ideally, you'd also include something like, 'I'm motivated to take care of myself because I'm fundamentally worthwhile and deserve to be well.' When you're engaged in self-care activities, do your three circles feel balanced? Next time you're engaging in an activity to take care of your wellbeing, do a quick check-in and imagine what your three circles would look like.

What helps you to soothe yourself? What types of activities help you to feel calm and content? Perhaps it's some soothing breathing, speaking kindly to yourself or engaging in an activity that you can immerse yourself in. This can be different for everybody. Are there people in your life who help you feel calm, content and connected? Some people find being with others soothing, assuming they are enjoyable people to be around! Some people find disengaging and being alone more effective for soothing. Think about what activates your soothing system and perhaps you can plan to do more of those activities. We'll be looking at ways you can engage in helpful activities later.

Does knowing that everyone suffers at times help you take care of yourself when you're struggling? Saying to yourself, 'There are other people who suffer like this. I'm not alone in this.' can help, but it's important this doesn't become a critical tone telling you that there are people suffering more than you and your suffering doesn't matter. That's minimisation of your suffering, more likely to activate your threat system and definitely not the point of self-care and compassion. There will always be people who suffer more than you and there will always be people who suffer less. This isn't an exercise in comparison; it's an acknowledgment that as humans we suffer, and we are not alone in that fact.

Even if your mind tells you that you don't take care of yourself, there are things you are doing that are taking care of you, no matter how small. When you're engaging in ways to take care of yourself, it can be helpful to simply ask yourself, 'What is motivating me to take whatever action I might be wanting to take?' If we can be aware of the motivation, we are far more likely to make helpful and compassionate choices.

## *Pause*

Take a moment and think about what motivates you to take care of yourself? You will likely have multiple motivations. List them all.

*Avoiding discomfort does not pave the path to a meaningful life.*

*Committed compassionate action can lead you where you want to go.*

# 2

# *Caring for All of You*

You may have heard terms like 'parts', 'younger self' or 'inner child'. There are many different frameworks and theories used to describe the concept of what I will be referring to as 'multiple selves'. I'm not talking about what used to be known as multiple personality disorder (now dissociative identity disorder). I'm talking about the fact that we are not merely one version of ourselves. We have many different parts of self.

Multiple selves is a term used in CFT to help people relate to the different versions of the self. When we can understand that we have differing emotions, motivations and responses, it allows us to shift perspective and offer ourselves a new way of relating to ourselves that can be kinder, more compassionate and ultimately more helpful.

Here's an example to illustrate what I mean. Bring to mind the last time you were invited to a social event. Was there a part of you that was looking forward to going and seeing your friends and another part of you that would rather stay home, watch your favourite show and have an early night? Or perhaps a time you were offered a new job or project, part of you may have been excited, whilst another part of you may have been feeling anxious and uncertain. Can you see how you're not just one version of yourself? The more you can understand and acknowledge this, the more you'll be able to take care of your different needs.

It's important to note that emotions and feelings are not mutually exclusive, meaning you can hold various emotions/feelings and even conflicting emotions/feelings at the same time. Each of our varied emotions comes with thoughts, behaviours, physical states, attentional focus, motivations and attached memories. In different situations, with different people, and under different circumstances, we interact differently. You likely relate differently to a friend, a parent or child, a spouse, an employer or a client. It would be a bit strange if you didn't. You would also act and feel differently when under pressure, threat or distressed by a situation, compared to when you are having fun or taking time out to relax.

### *Pause*

I invite you to bring to mind a situation where
you felt distressed or disturbed by something. Nothing too distressing. Maybe a score of five out of ten for distress.

- *During that experience, how did you take care of your own feelings?*
- *Was there space for your humanness?*
- *Did you take time to slow down and reflect on what you needed or how you could prepare yourself for whatever you had to do next?*

## CARING FOR ALL OF YOU

It's not unusual for us to neglect the parts of ourselves that are suffering in the moment. You can hope that you remember to tend to your feelings and needs later, but the more likely scenario is that you'll be busy with something else by then and those feelings and needs will be easily overlooked. Now imagine that happens once, then it happens every day or every week and this goes on for weeks, months, even years. An accumulation of moments of self-neglect. Not self-neglect that is necessarily noticeable. You may still be showering, eating, exercising, socialising with friends and doing the things that you know are helpful to you, or maybe you're not doing those things. I'm talking about the ongoing suffering that you are experiencing throughout your daily life, the suffering that you don't label as suffering, the feelings and needs you push through and set aside.

There are parts of you that need your attention, parts of you that are being continually reminded that they don't matter and their needs are not important. Ultimately those parts of you will demand attention. You may be familiar with the saying, 'If you don't make time for your wellness, you'll be forced to make time for your illness.' I'm here to tell you, if you don't make time to nurture and attend to all parts of yourself, you are putting yourself at greater risk of burnout and making it harder to manage everything.

If we truly want to take care of ourselves, we need to embrace the whole of who we are, not only the parts we like, love or feel proud of, but also our shadow side, often referred to as our dark side. Rest assured, we all have a shadow side. Our shadow side is the part of us that has dark thoughts, shameful feelings and is snarky, bitchy and uncaring. It is vengeful, spiteful and everything we like to think we are not or could never be. It is not all of who we are, but it is a part of who we are. It is important to acknowledge that as humans we are capable of awful and horrific acts. But just because we have the capacity to do something, doesn't mean we will choose to. However, if we don't recognise and acknowledge this, then when a dark or negative thought enters our mind, we might react to ourselves in an unnecessarily harsh and critical way. Alternatively in those moments, we can remind ourselves that this is all part of being human, that we did not choose our tricky mind, and that it's not our fault. This allows us to bring a more compassionate response to ourselves in those moments and gives us the opportunity to move forward in a way we would prefer.

I have a past just like you do. Some of it I look back on with joy and pride, and some of it I look back on and it makes me cringe or feel a sense of shame. Earlier in my life, I was very unhappy, and I know that I didn't always treat people in the way I would choose to treat them now. In fact, sometimes when I think about my younger self or I'm talking with someone about something from my past, I feel like I'm speaking about a different person. Sometimes I barely recognise myself in those stories. Through my journey of compassion, I am grateful that I'm able to recognise my own suffering during that time and acknowledge for myself that I spent a lot of time in my threat system. I now know that when we're in our threat system, we tend to be hostile to ourselves and others.

*Even hedgehogs need hugs,
even though they're prickly.*

When I was younger, I remember someone saying this to me and I now understand that I was the hedgehog in that scenario. When we feel hurt or scared, one of our responses, just like hedgehogs, is to raise our 'metaphorical' prickles as a way to protect ourselves from further threat. For us humans, it might look like being rude, abusive, saying mean or sarcastic things, resorting to physical violence, dismissing others' feelings or creating a defensive barrier by being stand-offish.

I have learnt to recognise my shadow side and appreciate that she needs care and compassion just as much as other parts of me. I've figured I'd be better off befriending this part of me because everywhere I go, she goes too. If you keep trying to avoid or deny parts of yourself, you'll never truly care for yourself in all the ways you need.

We must learn to accept that all of our feelings are valid, even the ones we don't like. We can make space for our humanness and understand how we engage in the world. We need to take the time to slow down and reflect on what our needs are and how we can prepare ourselves for the roles and work in our lives. What happens if we don't do this? We can neglect the parts of Self that are suffering at different times throughout the day. The problem with that is, when we are not caring for all parts of Self, we are not caring for ourselves in a deeply courageous way that creates sustainable wellbeing.

What happens when those parts of you that bring discomfort show up? Do you listen or avoid? How do you end up feeling when you neglect those parts of yourself? For example, maybe it's your angry self, and each time you ignore or shut down that part of you or try to avoid the pain that part of you feels, there's a push back and then it's hardly surprising you can end up behaving in ways you don't want to. You can forget that your angry self needs care too.

## Pause

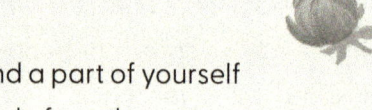

I now invite you to bring to mind a part of yourself that you are particularly critical of or reluctant to pay attention to.

- What comes up for you when you think about caring for that part of you?
- What are some beliefs you hold or stories you tell yourself about that part of you?
- Think about where those beliefs came from. Have these been passed to you from someone else?
- Are these beliefs helpful in allowing you to take care of your whole self?

You might be holding some pretty unhelpful stories and beliefs. We all do. There's a part of you that is ready and waiting to share those with you at any opportunity. You know the one – the critical voice that always likes to pop up uninvited. Let's go and find out more about that.

## The bully inside your brain

The sneaky inner critic, we've all got one, so let's get to know yours. The more you can recognise the parts of you that are trying (or succeeding) to take over the driving seat of your life, the more opportunity you have to choose whether that is helpful or harmful. If you can recognise when your critic is showing up, you can take a moment to reflect on why this might have happened. Then you can do your best to tend to any needs a part of you might have (likely fear based remember) and make a choice from a different part of you, a grounded and more compassionate part of you. We will get to know this part of you in the next section.

There is always a function to what you do, and self-criticism has a number of different possible functions. You might be someone who grew up with a lot of criticism from others, and self-criticism has developed as your primary motivation to ensure you 'get things right'. You might have experienced a parent who was frightening or abusive, and self-blame became your way of managing that situation. When you can understand what the function of your self-critic is, you can start to be more understanding and compassionate to yourself.

Many of us start off thinking that the critical part of ourselves is actually helping. It motivates us, right? Well, in some ways this can feel true. However, there are far more helpful and effective ways to motivate ourselves. Spoiler alert: self-compassion is not only more effective, it's also much nicer to engage in.

But wait, you say, 'Self-criticism stops me from being lazy, failing or getting hurt.' You're not alone in your thinking. Many people share these thoughts and believe that if they stop listening to their critic, those fears will become reality and they'll be rejected, negatively judged and ultimately end up alone. I've also had people say to me, 'I'll connect to my deeper feelings, and realise I don't want to.' I get it; that can feel scary. Even if you perceive your self-critic is in some way helping you, it's doing it in a way that is causing you pain and suffering. It is keeping you stuck in your threat system and impacting your quality of life. It can be a complex relationship that we have with our self-critic. We may want to ignore it and push it away. That's understandable. It's like having a bully coming towards you. You're hardly likely to embrace that situation and race up to them for a chat or want to give them a hug. But here's another problem: when we try to ignore something, it can just become a bigger problem.

So, what happens when your self-critic shows up? Do you listen to that voice in your head, or do you try to push it away and avoid it? You can forget that just like your angry self we spoke about before, your critical self needs your care too. This part of you has developed through your life experiences and is a response from your threat system.

Ask yourself if would you exclude someone in a group from engaging in a self-care activity because you didn't really like them? I very much doubt it. So why do you do that to parts of yourself! When you push away a part of you, there's no way that you can meet your needs in that moment. Instead, you can do your best to slow down and be curious about why your self-critic has shown up, why your threat system has been activated, and consider what you might need in that moment to feel a sense of safeness. So, I ask, is your self-critic really protecting you or is this a threat-system response that needs your attention? Let's take a look and see what's really going on and how it makes you feel. When thinking about that critical part of you, the following questions might help you to understand the function of your self-critic and why it shows up in the way that it does.

## *Pause*

Take some time to reflect on these questions. I want you to get to know your self-critic, so you can decide whether you want to keep listening to it or not. I have given some examples, but your self-critic might look and sound different.

- *When I imagine my self-critic, how would I describe what it looks like? (E.g. This could be a person-like figure, an animal, a shape or a colour – whatever makes sense for you)*
- *What are some of the things my self-critic says to me? (E.g. You're such a loser, you never finish anything you start, you're a burden, you're so disgusting, you're a fraud, you don't deserve XYZ, you'll never fit in, no one really loves you – yes, these are real examples of how my self-critic used to speak to me)*
- *How do I think my self-critic feels about me? (E.g. Disgusted, disappointed, angry, ashamed)*
- *What do I think my self-critic is trying to do? (E.g. Push me harder, keep me small, stop me from speaking out)*
- *How do I feel when my self-critic shows up? (E.g. Scared, sad, powerless, helpless, unmotivated)*
- *Do I still think my self-critic is helpful?*

I mentioned earlier that there's also a compassionate part of you. You might not be familiar with this part of yourself yet, or maybe you've started to connect more with your compassionate self. Either way, let's go and meet them now because that part of you can be really helpful when your self-critic shows up.

## The best friend that's right there waiting for you

Your compassionate self is the part of you that is wise, strong, courageous and motivated to care for you and others. In my opinion, they're like the best friend you could hope for. For me, cultivating my compassionate self has been absolutely life changing and I don't say that lightly. It has taken a lot of reflection and willingness to take action to change my relationship with myself, and all I can say is, it's most definitely been worth it.

That part of me has always been there; I just didn't give her the time of day. It wasn't until I was forced to stop due to burnout and ill health, and I allowed myself to slow down, that I started to hear her more clearly. To be honest, I felt so awful that I was desperate for anything that could help me feel better about myself and my situation. So, I started to listen to what she was saying to me. With the help of other caring, compassionate and supportive people, I was able to learn what I needed to learn, and take action that would prove to be so much more helpful than tuning in to the playlist in my head that was stuck on 'Critical Radio'.

You may already be in touch with your compassionate self, or they may be more like a stranger to you right now. Either way, it can be helpful to spend some time thinking about this part of you, so let's do that now. Remember, you can always come back to this later if that suits you better. We will also continue to explore your compassionate self and compassionate responses throughout the book. For now, let's get curious about your compassionate self, the same way you did with your self-critic.

## *Pause*

Take some time to reflect on the following questions. This is your opportunity to get to know your compassionate self.

- *What do I imagine my compassionate self would look like? (E.g. This could be a person-like figure, an animal, a shape or a colour – whatever makes sense for you, even if it changes)*
- *What are some things my compassionate self would say to me? (E.g. You're doing the best you can, I know it's hard, I feel your pain, I'm proud of you, you've always been enough, what do you need, I love you darling – these are real-life examples of how my compassionate self speaks to me – quite the change from my self-critic, don't you think!)*
- *How do I think my compassionate self feels about me? (E.g. Acceptance, empathy, positive regard, tenderness)*
- *How would my compassionate self behave towards me? (E.g. Support me, hug me, speak kindly to me, encourage me, celebrate me, nurture me)*
- *When I imagine my compassionate self, what does this part want to help me with? How does it want to guide me? (E.g. Encourage me to do my best, motivate me to take care of myself, be understanding of my challenges, allow me to access my wisdom)*
- *How do I feel when I think about my compassionate self? (E.g. Calmer, more grounded, stronger, understood, loved, motivated)*
- *Do I think my compassionate self is helpful?*

How did you go with that exercise? I know it can be hard at first. Another way to engage with your compassionate self is through imagery and meditation. We will explore that next.

*In this moment I invite*
*My most compassionate self*
*To sit with me*
*To hold me*
*To guide me*

## Compassionate imagery

It's important to know that people have varied experiences when it comes to imagery and meditations. There is no right or wrong way to engage in these practices. What is important is that you engage in a way that feels helpful for you and that you know at any point you can choose to leave the practice and return to it if and when you decide.

You may be someone who can clearly and vividly bring images to mind, or you might be someone who experiences through colour, sensation or with a feeling or a knowing. Some people have a condition called *aphantasia* – an inability to visualise images in your mind. I am someone who struggles to visualise with my eyes closed. I have a strong felt sense of what I am imagining and that sometimes comes with tiny fleeting blobs of colours or blurry images. I find it much easier to bring an image to mind when my eyes are open, which to be honest, I do find a little confusing. I used to feel stressed when people gave instructions about imagining. I felt somehow defective because I wasn't drawing pictures in my mind, yet I could clearly describe what I was sensing. I would pretend and mask my true experience due to the shame that arose for me. Now I accept that this is how my imagining happens. It's how my mind works, and I've grown to appreciate it.

Whatever way you experience this is unique to you and in no way wrong. All I ask is that you always check in with yourself and engage to the level that feels right for you in the moment. That level of engagement might change each time you do a practice, or it might stay the same. That's all 'normal'. Although a dear client once said to me, 'Normal is just a setting on a washing machine.' That always makes me smile, and I couldn't agree more. How you experience something is your experience, and it's valid.

## FROM SELF-NEGLECT TO SELF-COMPASSION

If you're anything like me, you probably like to know what's coming next, so let me give you a rundown of what I'm about to take you through. We will spend a short time engaging in a breathing technique called Soothing Rhythm Breathing, a practice developed by Professor Paul Gilbert. Soothing Rhythm Breathing is a key exercise used to slow down your body and mind, which in turn allows you more choice in how you respond to internal and external stress. This is a breathing technique that involves your body, breath, inner voice and facial expressions to support you in activating your soothing system (green circle). After this first guided meditation, you have the opportunity to reflect on your experience, and then I invite and guide you to connect with your compassionate self and tune in to your wisdom regarding what you need.

Remember, there is no 'right' way. Find what works for you. You're more likely to benefit from these exercises if they don't feel like yet another task on the list of things to do! Perhaps see this as an opportunity to give TO yourself rather than place an expectation ON yourself. If you believe this is helpful, then you're more likely to have better outcomes.

Exercises like this are a practice. It takes time to establish a rhythm and routine. There's no expectation that you'll find this easy at first, and even when it does get easier, you'll have times when it feels harder again. Every time you practise, even briefly, you will move towards a different way of relating to yourself, and away from doing things that perhaps aren't currently working for you. One other thing: don't expect that you'll clear your mind. That's not how your mind works. It saddens me when I hear that people give up on mindfulness or meditation because they can't quieten their minds. Of course you can't. Minds are for thinking and think they will, so let your mind do what your mind will do and just be curious and aware of that.

You might like to record yourself reading this so you can then close your eyes and play it back. Alternatively, you can use the QR code, and I will guide you. I offer the option to record yourself and hear your own voice during the meditation as I found that to be a very helpful way of cultivating my own compassionate voice. Hearing myself say the words as I sat quietly was another way for me to practise developing an internal compassionate voice. This might be something you also find helpful. Choose whatever works best for you. You can always do both options and see which suits you better.

> These scripts have been adapted with permission from *The Compassionate Mind Workbook*, by Chris Irons and Elaine Beaumont, Robinson 2017.

Let's start with a short practice of Soothing Rhythm Breathing and then we will move on to a compassionate imagery practice.

## SOOTHING RHYTHM BREATHING

*I invite you to find a comfortable position, ideally with your feet on the floor, in an upright position allowing an open diaphragm. You can open your diaphragm by gently rolling your shoulders up and back. Most important is that you listen to what your body needs and give yourself permission to do that. It might be sitting on a chair or the floor, laying down on the floor or your bed, or any other position that suits you. Honour your body in a way that feels comfortable. Take a moment to give yourself permission to experience this in whatever way it unfolds and know that at any time, you can choose to come out of this practice and return to it as you desire.*

*If it feels comfortable, go ahead and close your eyes, or gently rest your gaze at a spot in front of you. Begin by adopting a friendly facial expression, perhaps a half smile. Now I invite you to bring your attention to your breath. Notice the sensations that are present as you breathe in and breathe out. If you notice that your attention becomes distracted and moves away from your breath, try not to judge. This is perfectly normal; it is what our mind does. See if you can just observe that this is happening and gently try to bring your attention back to your breathing. Notice your in-breath and your out-breath.*

*Notice the rise and fall of your belly and your chest as you breathe in and as you breathe out.*

*As you settle your attention on your breath, gently deepen and slow down your breath to find a soothing rhythm that feels natural and comfortable. If your mind wanders again, remember you have a choice. You can follow your mind where it wants to take you or you can gently return your attention to the soothing rhythm of your breath.*

*Now see if you can slow down your breathing a little further. Try breathing in for the count of three and out for the count of three. If this feels okay, then start to slow down your breath to a count of four on the in-breath and four on the out-breath for the next few breaths. And now, if you can, slow it down a little more to a count of five on the in-breath and 5 on the out-breath. If this feels too slow for you, find a rhythm that feels right for you in this moment. If it feels too fast, you can try breathing in for the count of six and out for the count of six. Just allow your breath to find its own soothing rhythm of equal in-breaths and out-breaths.*

*On the next out-breath, you might like to use a friendly, calm voice tone and say to yourself: Mind slowing down … And on the next out-breath say to yourself: Body slowing down …*

*I invite you to spend a few more moments with your breath, just noticing the in-breath and the out-breath and how your body and mind are feeling.*

*Now start to notice the sounds around you. Gently guide your attention to how it feels to be sitting or lying where you are. Gently make some small movements with your fingers and toes. As you feel ready, you can open your eyes, bring your attention back to the place you are in and stretch your body or give your body whatever it needs right now.*

Now you've experienced Soothing Rhythm Breathing, take a moment to reflect on how different the pace, depth and rhythm of your breath was compared to the way you usually breathe, and how that felt for you.

As we move into the compassionate self imagery, I invite you to start the meditation by engaging your Soothing Rhythm Breathing. Let's now use our tricky mind in a way that can be really helpful: imagining your most compassionate self. Again, you might like to record yourself reading this so you can then close your eyes and play it back. Alternatively, you can use the QR code, and I will guide you.

## COMPASSIONATE SELF IMAGERY

*I invite you to find a comfortable position, ideally with your feet on the floor, in an upright position allowing an open diaphragm. You can open your diaphragm by gently rolling your shoulders up and back. Most important is that you listen to what your body needs and give yourself permission to do that. It might be sitting on a chair or the floor, laying down on the floor or your bed, or any other position that suits you. Honour your body in a way that feels comfortable. I will be inviting you to imagine different things and for some people, imagining looks different. It doesn't matter whether you bring to mind complete images, partial images or even just a felt sense of what is being described. Take a moment to give yourself permission to experience this in whatever way this unfolds for you and know that at any time, you can choose to come out of this practice and return to it as you desire.*

*Go ahead and engage in Soothing Rhythm Breathing and allow yourself to settle into a rhythm that feels good for you. Now you're going to use your imagination to create what it would feel like if you were your most compassionate self. I invite you to think about some of the qualities of your ideal compassionate self.*

*First, consider the quality of wisdom. You understand that we have tricky brains that we did not choose for ourselves but were created over millions of years of evolution. You understand that many of the circumstances of your early life experiences involved decisions you did not make. You understand that you are doing the best you can under the circumstances you are in, with the skills, knowledge and resources that you have. Imagine as best you can how it feels to be this wise self with a deep understanding of how hard life can be and knowing that all human beings face struggles throughout life. How does this feel in your body? How do you interact with yourself and others?*

*Second, consider the quality of strength and courage. Your compassionate self has an inner strength and confidence. A courage to attend to the pain and suffering experienced by yourself and others. It is grounded and can tolerate distress. Notice how being strong and courageous feels in your body. How do you hold your body? How do you stand with a sense of confidence and strength?*

*Finally, consider the quality of a caring commitment, a deep desire to be kind, caring and supportive in the world. A commitment to preventing and alleviating suffering, both for yourself and others. Imagine having these qualities and how it feels in your body. Consider what your body posture is like and what your facial expression looks like. What does your tone of voice sound like?*

*Now, holding on to your sense of wisdom, your courage and strength, and your motivation to be caring, recognise that you have a deep intention to be sensitive to suffering, a desire to try to be supportive and to alleviate distress. Really notice how this feels inside. Imagine how you move, what your facial expression is like, what your voice tone sounds like.*

*Now I invite you to place a hand or both hands over your heart. Notice your breath and if you need to, gently slow down your breathing. Next, imagine that you are looking through the eyes of your compassionate self at a version of yourself: the you that is doing your best to navigate the world. Take a moment to look at yourself with care and kindness. Perhaps give yourself a warm smile. Notice your deep desire for this version of you to find peace, comfort and a sense of wellbeing.*

*As you look at yourself, connect with your understanding that life can be challenging and stressful, and that you are doing your best under the circumstances you are in, with the skills, knowledge and resources you currently have. See if you can feel empathy for this everyday version of yourself.*

*Now think about what your compassionate self wants to say to you. You may find it helpful to use a warm voice tone and offer yourself the following words:*

> *May I be at ease.*
> *May I feel safe.*
> *May I feel grounded and calm.*
> *May I meet myself with kindness.*
> *May I meet my challenges with strength, courage and wisdom.*
>
> *Now take a moment to notice your breath, and if you need to slow it down, then slow it down. Notice how it feels when you're connected to your compassionate self. As best you can, remember to be non-judgemental and curious. If your mind wanders, gently bring your attention back to your breath. I invite you to spend a few more moments with your breath, just noticing the in-breath and the out-breath.*
>
> *Now start to notice the sounds around you. Gently guide your attention to how it feels to be sitting or lying where you are. Gently make some small movements with your fingers and toes. As you feel ready, you can open your eyes, bring your attention back to the place you are in and stretch your body or give your body whatever it needs right now.*

Now you've had the opportunity to try to connect with your compassionate self, take some time to reflect on your experience. Notice I said *try to* connect. You might have found it hard to connect with that part of you. That's okay. This is a practice, and you can try again.

- Did you find it easy or hard to slow down and engage in Soothing Rhythm Breathing?
- Did you find it easy or hard to connect to your compassionate self?

- What stood out for you most about this experience?
- What did you learn about yourself during this experience?

You can choose to practise this once a day, or if that seems too much right now, maybe aim for three times a week or whatever feels right for you to start.

> **QUICK TIP:** As an ADHDer, I find it helpful to set reminders in my phone when starting a new practice, otherwise, even with all the best intentions in the world, I forget!

I hope what we've covered so far has given you an opportunity to start to reflect and get to know yourself a little better. Understanding that you are a human with a tricky mind, and a whole variety of experiences that have shaped who you are, allows you to start connecting with yourself in a more compassionate way. It allows you to be more forgiving when you make mistakes which of course, we all do. It can assist you to be gentler with yourself when you are suffering and helps motivate you towards what is helpful when you need some encouragement.

Being aware of the sorts of narratives and messaging in the world can help normalise some of the thoughts and feelings you have and give you a chance to reflect and change your perspective on how you want to engage with yourself and others. You are not just one version of yourself, but a whole that is made up of many parts with different needs and wants. Recognising this allows you to make a choice to tend to your needs as they arise in more helpful ways. This allows you to nurture and care for your whole self rather than neglect parts of you that you either don't recognise or don't want to attend to.

## Understanding self-neglect

My choice to study psychology and work in a profession that is focused on the service and wellbeing of others absolutely helped me to learn so much about myself, about being human, and the sheer resilience of humanity. It also gave me a deep sense of meaning. My time as a psychologist, and the opportunity to work with the clients that trusted me with their stories, vulnerabilities and glimpses into their lives and strengths, is something I will always be so grateful for and humbled by.

'The best way to find yourself is to lose yourself in the service of others' is a sentiment widely attributed to Gandhi, though its origin is unclear. I say, you must not stay lost. You can't only be in service to others. This is not about being selfish or fully connected to your ego, but about the need to find yourself through that process, so you can learn to also be of service to yourself.

Self-neglect can start early in life. Perhaps you had a caregiver who wasn't resourced enough or capable of meeting your needs in an appropriate way and you learnt to abandon those needs. Maybe your early life circumstances led you to being a caregiver for the person who was meant to be your caregiver. It might have been that your caregiver(s) did the best they could but inadvertently dismissed your feelings or never explicitly talked to you about how to recognise and express your emotions and needs. However this self-abandonment and self-neglect developed for you, you might now find yourself behaving in ways that reinforce the importance of other people's needs and minimisation of your own.

Self-neglect can range from minor moments of ignoring your needs through to ignoring your health needs, personal hygiene, living requirements and anything in between. What I'm talking about here is the disconnection from yourself and your needs, whether these be physical, emotional or practical in nature. It makes sense that this self-neglect happens, particularly for women. You have grown up in a patriarchal, capitalist society that has been full of messaging that you are not as valuable as others, that you are meant for service and caring for others. From a young age, you've likely had messaging that taught you to push your own needs aside for the sake of someone else and, as you continued to grow, these messages remained and may have even become stronger.

This is not your fault, but the hard truth is no one is going to make those changes for you. Nor do you need them to. You're an amazing person and have the strength and courage within you to make the changes you need to make, even if you don't yet feel like you do. It's likely plenty of people are benefiting from your self-neglect, and it sure isn't you. Let's get explicit about what self-neglect might look like.

Here are some examples:

- Skipping meals because 'they' need your attention
- Packing lunches for 'them' only to realise you don't have any lunch for yourself
- Feeling upset about a situation and then minimising the impact it has on you
- Minimising the importance of something you plan to do
- Never celebrating your achievements
- Staying in a job you dread
- Organising activities for everyone else and having no time for the activities you enjoy
- Continuing to come up with reasons why your partner treats you the way they do, rather than acknowledging you're

unhappy (or unsafe) and deep down knowing you deserve better
- Year upon year pushing back your dream of starting your own business, changing your career, travelling or whatever your dream is
- Taking loved ones to health appointments but not having regular or necessary health check-ups yourself
- Missing important life meetings
- Not getting your hair done even though you want to
- Buying treats and gifts for others, but never treating yourself
- Always tending to the needs of others even when it comes at the expense of your health, happiness and wellbeing

Do any of these feel familiar? I imagine you're nodding along to at least some of these.

What are some more that you can think of for yourself?

Ask yourself this: what will happen if nothing changes? Often, people end up feeling resentful, angry, anxious, depressed, hopeless. If you keep pouring into others and giving nothing to yourself, I can almost guarantee that is a recipe for dissatisfaction and burnout.

## The high cost of burnout

Despite it being so important, I hear people saying, 'I probably should take care of myself better because then I'll be able to take care of my clients, children, family better.' Why does your self-care always have to be in service of caring for anyone else, or connected to the wellbeing of anyone else? What if you could take care of yourself because that is what you need and what you deserve, purely because you are a human being trying to navigate life?

Now I'm not saying that taking care of each other isn't important. In fact, I think community care is an essential part of self-care. However, it's so easy for women to make self-care and taking care of their needs dependent on them being able to take care of others more effectively, rather than about them deserving care and nurturance.

I run groups for women, and I've noticed that even in a space that is dedicated to personal practice and self-care, the conversation easily turns towards what our clients, partners, children and others in our life need. Why is it so hard for us to turn care towards ourselves? Where did we get lost in this? What did we hear in our earlier lives or somewhere along the way that told us, 'Other people matter more than you do'? Yes, your family, friends, clients and community matter. Yes, the way you engage personally and professionally with people is important, and spoiler alert: you really matter too. Why am I so passionate about this? Because burnout is real and can be devastating. It hurts so many aspects of your life (and the lives of those around you too). It can take everything you have and all that you are and metaphorically burn it to the ground.

Burnout swept through my life like a forest fire and nearly took everything from me.

My health was significantly impacted, both physically and mentally, and some of those impacts have been long-lasting. My ability to work was affected and ultimately, I had to stop what I was doing for a period of time, and that meant a huge decrease in my earning capacity. This also created increased anxiety as it triggered memories of being a solo parent struggling financially and I felt heavily dependent on my new husband. This added to my stress and distress as I had been financially dependent in a previous relationship. I had to keep reminding myself that my new relationship was safe and supportive, but it was tough. My relationships, both intimate and social, were compromised. I feared losing friendships as I continually declined invitations or had to change plans at the last minute due to feeling so unwell. Mostly, I feared that my current state of health and capacity would lead to my husband deciding that I wasn't worth being with. He assures me this thought never once crossed his mind. Quite the opposite, he continually looked for ways he could support me and make my life easier. That didn't stop my self-critic from showing up and telling me what a waste of space I was and that I'd soon end up alone. Yes, even though I was a trained psychologist, I ended up in a dark spiral fuelled by the flames of burnout and the societal messages that I had to be productive to be worthwhile.

I want to help you recognise the signs and symptoms of burnout, understand the risk factors in your life and bring awareness to the things that can help protect you. This is essential information if you want to truly take care of yourself and avoid the slippery slope of burnout. Don't be tempted to skip over this part.

## So, what actually is burnout?

The construct of burnout was first proposed in 1974 by American psychologist Herbert Freudenberger. He described burnout as a state of emotional, mental, and often physical exhaustion caused by prolonged or repeated stress (in the context of a workplace). We also know that burnout can occur in many settings outside of work, e.g. parenting, managing chronic health, committing to too many committees/activities, and/or being neurodivergent in a world designed for a neurotypical mind. I was born in the 1970s, and it saddens and angers me that fifty-plus years later, we are still having conversations about the increasing rates of burnout. According to multiple studies, the rates are getting worse, not better, with between 50% and 82% of Australian workers, and up to 90% of unpaid carers, experiencing burnout. There are, of course, many systemic issues contributing to this.

Let's take a look at the most common signs and symptoms of burnout. You might recognise yourself in a few, or a lot, of the following and this can be confronting. Please go gently with yourself and remember there is help available.

Three main symptoms were described by Maslach and Jackson in 1976:

1) Feelings of energy depletion or exhaustion
2) Feelings of negativity or cynicism related to your job [or other domain], or increased mental distance from your job [or another domain]
3) Reduced sense of professional [or personal] efficacy

Other symptoms can include:

- Self-doubt
- Procrastinating/taking longer to get things done
- Feeling overwhelmed
- Withdrawing from responsibilities
- Isolating yourself from others
- Feeling helpless, trapped and/or defeated
- Feeling detached/alone in the world

- Using food, drugs or alcohol to cope
- Taking out your frustrations on others
- Skipping work or coming in late and leaving early
- Avoiding tasks
- Insomnia
- Difficulty concentrating
- Headaches, nausea and other illnesses
- Anxiety
- Depression

The risk factors of burnout include:

- Your own experiences throughout life
- Early childhood trauma
- Trauma across your lifetime
- Current stressors
- Client/customer/personal load too high or too full of problems
- Problematic boundaries/sense of over-responsibility
- Limited support at and outside of work/toxic workplace culture
- Seeing work or roles as your identity

The protective factors for burnout prevention include:

- Healthy boundaries – not too loose or too rigid
- Good time management – challenging for many ADHDers
- Intentional energy management
- Being aware of client/customer/personal load – intentional diary management
- Finding meaning in your work/role

- A sense of autonomy
- Having opportunities for professional development to maintain a sense of competency
- Adequate support in and outside of work
- Having interests outside work
- Personal development work – like reading this book

For the neurodivergent folks among us, burnout often results from trying to continually navigate a neurotypical world. It can manifest in different ways that might include difficulty with emotional regulation, increased sensory sensitivity, a decreased ability to manage daily functioning and/or an increased need for disengagement or alone time.

When you mask who you are and what you're experiencing – and constantly deny your needs – this can be very draining. It does not stop burnout from happening; it just covers it up and delays the inevitable! If you are constantly exposed to overwhelming sensory stimuli and don't have the accommodations you need, this can lead to increased stress and contribute to burnout. If, like me, you have ADHD, you are constantly managing your focus, attention and executive functioning (the ability to plan, prioritise, organise, implement your thoughts and take action) which can be really tiring. On top of these inherent challenges, you might be blaming yourself for needing accommodations, and your sneaky self-critic might be giving you a hard time for not 'coping'.

Being born as a human with a tricky mind isn't your fault, but if you want life to be different, you need to understand that it is your responsibility to understand yourself in a way that can assist you to make different choices.

## It's not your fault; it is your responsibility

As I wrote earlier, why would we choose a mind that gets caught up in worry, rumination, social comparison, self-doubt, catastrophising and so much more that holds us back and leaves us feeling less than and not good enough? We do not choose so many of our earlier (and later) experiences.

You didn't choose the country you were born in or the parents who birthed you. You didn't choose your caregivers as you navigated the early years. You didn't choose your eye colour, skin colour, hair colour, gender or sexuality. You weren't the one who chose where you lived, how you were educated, what you ate or who you spent a lot of your time with. Of course, as you get older, your autonomy increases, and different choices are available to you. It's important to recognise, though, that those early experiences and socialisation impact the choices you make as you age.

> *While not everyone will relate to this specific example, it shows how even behaviours that later cause us pain can begin as ways to cope when we have limited choices. The same can apply to many less visible struggles.

> *I remember a client I worked with many years ago. She was struggling with drug addiction and trying hard to make changes in her life that would help her feel calmer, safer and more engaged in a life she wanted for herself. She constantly blamed herself for being addicted to drugs. Her self-critic was brutal and unforgiving. I'll never forget the conversation we had talking about her early life experiences and how little choice she had at that point. She agreed she wouldn't have chosen a lot*

*of the circumstances and experiences she had when she was little. We also spoke about her tricky mind and how it looked for anything that would take her pain away and help her feel safe. For her, that was drugs.*

*I asked her if she had always dreamed of being a drug addict. She looked at me and said that obviously she didn't! We spoke about drugs being a solution to a problem at a time when she had such limited choices. We spoke about the choices she would like for her life and the dreams she did have when she was a young girl. Her realisation that she didn't choose to be addicted to drugs allowed her to let go of a lot of shame and connect with a compassionate part of herself that wanted to nurture and care for her.*

Recognising and letting go of self-blame and shame is key. It allows you to move out of your threat system and connect with your strong, wise, courageous compassionate self. From here you can make different decisions – decisions that are helpful, not harmful.

While it's not your fault that you have this tricky brain you didn't design or ask for, if you want things to be different, then it is your responsibility. It's your responsibility to understand who you are as a human being, what has impacted you and how you impact others. It is up to you to take responsibility for what you do next. Now this is of course a choice. Not everyone wants to do the work it takes to gain the understanding, or the work it takes to learn new ways of doing things, and then practise doing it differently. You're reading this book, so I'd say there's a good chance you are ready to take that responsibility and do the work, and I'm so happy for you.

We've looked at your tricky brain and the fact that you are multiple versions of self. You've gotten curious about your inner critic and started to explore your compassionate self. We've talked about self-neglect and the burnout that can result from that. We've acknowledged that it's not your fault, but it is your responsibility if you want things to be different. Let's now look at your emotions, because they play a big part in your human experience, even if you're someone who doesn't easily recognise your emotions or feel comfortable expressing them. Whether you do or don't, they're still there impacting how you think, feel and behave.

*What if life isn't about pushing
away all the discomfort?*

*But instead making space for it.
And treating yourself with the
compassion you deserve.*

# 3

# *Making Sense of Feelings and the Beliefs that Hold You Back*

Now of course you experience many more than three emotions, but here we're going to be focusing on the three most talked about in CFT: anxiety, anger and sadness. Often, people connect or express more easily with one or two of these, and avoid or don't even recognise one or maybe two as emotions they possess.

This is an opportunity for you to pause and reflect on how you experience each of these emotions.

When we understand how we experience, respond to and express our emotions, it gives us more opportunity to choose whether we want to continue with how this happens or make a choice to do things differently. It's difficult, if not impossible, to change something we're not aware of. It's easier to treat ourselves more compassionately when we understand 'the why' behind our behaviours. I invite you to bring an air of curiosity to these next reflections and try not to judge your thoughts and responses. Be as open and honest with yourself as you can and always go gently with yourself. You might want to answer the following questions in a notebook or just in your mind, whatever works best for you.

## Anxiety

Let's start with anxiety, as in my experience, this tends to be an emotion most of us are familiar with, even if you don't label it as anxiety. Anxiety is a feeling of unease, worry and fear and can range from mild to severe. It can be an expected and normal reaction to a situation and at times of mild stress, it can be helpful. It can also be extremely disruptive to your life and overall wellbeing, if persistent and unmanaged.

Anxiety comes with a range of symptoms, including:

- Trouble sleeping
- Inability to remain calm
- Increased heart rate
- Dry mouth
- Feelings of panic or a sense of danger
- Sweaty palms
- Tingling in the hands or feet
- Shortness of breath or increased speed of breath
- Dizziness
- Inability to concentrate
- Constantly thinking about a problem or situation

## *Pause*

Take a moment to consider your thoughts about anxiety and how you treat yourself when you're feeling anxious.

- *Do you recognise your own anxiety?*
- *Do you recognise anxiety in other people?*
- *Is anxiety an 'acceptable' feeling for you?*
- *What shows up for you when you think about yourself or others being anxious?*
- *How do you manage your anxiety?*
- *How have other people responded to your anxiety?*
- *How do you respond to other people's anxiety?*
- *Are you able to be with yours or other people's anxiety?*

## Anger

Next, we're going to explore anger. This can often be a tricky one. As women, we've been socialised to think that anger is 'unbecoming'. It's not an emotion that is encouraged, quite the opposite. We're likely to be labelled hysterical, emotional, irrational, feisty, crazy or a nag.

A dear friend of mine has a teenage daughter, May. She is a smart, curious, engaging and compassionate person. During a visit I made to their home, I was fortunate to hear May practising a speech for a public speaking competition she was in. Her speech was about domestic violence and the tragedy of women's deaths in Australia. It was powerful, moving and also heartbreaking to hear a teenager speaking on such a topic. May felt angry. I felt angry. It is something we ought to be feeling angry about. After my visit, May went on to present her speech and at the end an adult came over to her and told her she was a 'funny one' and that she'd be a 'firecracker' when she's older. May was understandably angry about this response to her speech. There was nothing funny about what she spoke about. I have to wonder, if a male was presenting May's speech, would they find the same humour and be dismissive of the subject? Even during a speaking competition, where someone has been invited to speak out, girls and women find themselves dismissed, disrespected and invalidated, so it's hardly surprising that many women stay quiet. Society needs to do better. It is not good enough. Anger is a valid emotion for everyone, and we all have a right to express it in healthy ways.

Anger is a basic human emotion that we feel in response to unfairness, injustice, perceived threats or unmet needs. This might range from annoyance through to rage. Anger itself is not the problem; however, some expressions of anger can be problematic. If you've been raised by or are in a relationship with someone who expresses anger in a harmful way, this can lead to a fear of anger, and you being unwilling to acknowledge and express your own anger. Anger can be helpful in signalling to us that there is a problem with something or someone, that a need isn't being met or a boundary has been crossed. It can also serve as a motivator to change a situation or to protect ourselves or others. When acknowledged and expressed in healthy ways, anger can be a signpost worth paying attention to.

## *Pause*

Take a moment to consider your thoughts about anger and how you treat yourself when you're feeling angry.

- *Do you recognise your own anger?*
- *Do you recognise anger in other people?*
- *Is anger an 'acceptable' feeling for you?*
- *What shows up for you when you think about yourself or others being angry?*
- *How do you manage your anger?*
- *How do you manage your anger towards other people's behaviour/attitude?*
- *How have other people responded to your anger?*
- *How do you respond to other people's anger?*
- *Are you able to be with this range of feelings in yourself or others?*

## Sadness

Finally, we're going to explore sadness. Sadness isn't just about tears. It can show up in many ways, from a quiet sense of heaviness to wracking sobs that consume the whole of you. Sadness lets us know that something matters to us. It is a healthy emotion and also one that a lot of people struggle to express or would rather ignore. You might have grown up hearing things like 'don't be a cry-baby' or 'stop crying or I'll give you something to cry about'. Really not helpful in assisting us to recognise, acknowledge and express our emotions in a healthy way. You might have noticed that if you cry, you're handed a tissue very quickly and lovingly told, 'Don't cry.' You might take that as a sign that your tears aren't welcome or acceptable, or that other people can't tolerate your emotions. There are varied reasons why you might struggle with sadness, so let's look at that now.

## *Pause*

Take a moment to consider your thoughts about sadness and how you treat yourself when you're feeling sad.

- *Do you recognise your own sadness?*
- *Do you recognise sadness in other people?*
- *Is sadness an 'acceptable' feeling for you?*
- *What shows up for you when you think about yourself or others being sad?*
- *How do you manage your sadness?*
- *How have other people responded to your sadness?*
- *How do you respond to other people's sadness?*
- *Are you able to be with this feeling in yourself or others?*

What did you notice reflecting on those questions? Did you notice differences between the emotions? Are there ways you treat your emotions differently to the emotions of others? Are there emotions you find more acceptable? Are you more or less accepting of certain emotions in others? You can use these examples to generalise to other feelings you experience.

How we feel about something is one thing; what we believe is another. The beliefs we hold about ourselves and the situations we find ourselves in can be both helpful and harmful. They can encourage us forward or hold us back.

Let's take some time to explore the limiting beliefs you hold that are perhaps keeping you from thriving in the life you want.

## Limiting beliefs

Limiting beliefs really are what they say on the label. Beliefs you hold that limit you in some way or another. These might be beliefs you've held for many years, perhaps since childhood, or beliefs you've picked up along the way as you journey through life. The problem with some of these beliefs is they really don't serve you well. They can block your progress, fill you with self-doubt and sabotage your dreams.

It can be helpful to take some time to explore what beliefs you hold, where they came from and if they are helpful. Sometimes the beliefs you hold are internalised beliefs that you've heard from other people. Sometimes the beliefs you hold about yourself and/or your situation are true. This is not where you start with the toxic positivity and try to convince yourself that you can do anything and that everything is always going to be alright. Your experiences may have many aspects that are out of your control. You may have restrictions on your life that no matter how hard you try, you can't change. You may experience oppression, stigmatisation, and disadvantages that can't be undone by reading a book. If this is you, please go gently with yourself during this work. Be fair with yourself about your role in your situation. I imagine you will have some limiting beliefs that can be addressed, but please don't take misplaced responsibility for some of the parameters of your life that you didn't create and cannot control.

Let me start by introducing you to the word cage. We all have one, but they might sound different to each of us. Your word cage is full of those pesky negative statements and words you say to yourself, some of them so old and ingrained that you don't even recognise you're doing it. Taking time to reflect on how you speak to yourself really starts to highlight how you treat yourself, how you might feel about yourself and what might be getting in the way of you making the choices you want to make and living the life you want. It's important to think about your beliefs around self-care and your own wellbeing.

This mind is a sneaky little sucker and can get you stuck in all sorts of situations. One of the ways your mind can get in the way and sabotage your life is with the limiting beliefs you hold. You can get caught in a word cage of your own making. I'm not saying this is your fault; your word cage is built over time from an early age. It is the culmination of all the social interactions, experiences and input you've had across your lifetime. We all have some beliefs that don't serve us, but once upon a time they did. At some point, those beliefs either kept you safe or allowed you to do something that you didn't think you could. So, let's not spend time on regret. Instead, look at how you can uncover what they are, decide whether they still serve you and if they're no longer helpful, how to replace them with something that is.

I invite you to spend some time writing down your most troublesome words, phrases and thoughts. You know, the ones you often find on repeat in your mind. You might notice these show up more frequently or strongly when you are trying something new, meeting new people, taking action on a new idea or focusing on your own needs. Anything that starts to move you outside of your comfort zone will likely trigger these thoughts. It's a very natural reaction because your brain is designed to keep you safe, so that's what it's going to try to do, even if it's not actually helpful to you. If you've got a mind that is jam-packed with beliefs, you can come back to this later and keep adding to your list. Or you can stay with it until you feel like you've got them all. My guess is you'll think of some others later and you can add those to your list as you go.

## *Pause*

I invite you to pause and take a moment to write down what is in your word cage. I'll give you some prompts to get you started, but feel free to do this in a way that works for you. Write down the most troublesome words, phrases, and thoughts that you currently have or say to yourself.

> *Who am I to...*
> *What if...*
> *I can't...*
> *I'm so stupid*
> *If only...*
> *I never get it right*
> *I must...*
> *I'll always feel like this*
> *I should...*
> *Resting is lazy*
> *It's selfish to put myself first*

If you haven't heard the saying 'Don't should all over yourself', it's worth remembering because that 'shoulding' can be far more frequent than you think.

You might be surprised at how much you managed to write down. Maybe things showed up that surprised you, or perhaps it was all very familiar. There might be a lot in your word cage. I know mine used to be stuffed to the brim. There are still some in mine, of course. I don't think we can magically rid ourselves of all the unhelpful thoughts and beliefs we hold, but I do know that we can be aware of them and make choices about whether we allow them to rule our life. Now that you can see more clearly how you're interacting with yourself, how does it feel? This can be a tough realisation, so go gently with yourself and take a break if you need.

Would you speak to your family, friends, partner, children, colleagues or people out in public the way you speak to yourself? I'm guessing not. I know when I first did some of this work, I was shocked at how horrible, mean and abusive I was to myself and had been for decades of my life. And what's worse, it was always when I was struggling the most that I would be the harshest. Can you relate to that?

I want you to be able to break free from your word cage. It doesn't mean that these beliefs won't ever show up again, but you'll be more aware of them, and that allows you to choose how you want to respond when they do show up. You don't have to let the fears and self-doubt attached to these thoughts make the decisions for your life. You don't have to turn down opportunities because your tricky mind tells you it's too much, or you're not enough, or whatever it is your tricky mind is saying to you.

Let's now look at how we can break free from this. Yes, it is possible. You will likely take some time to make a big shift and find yourself falling back into patterns as you make these changes, but that's okay. Remember, it's a process and a practice.

I'll give you an example of how these sneaky little beliefs can show up, even when we think we've mastered them. I've been on top of managing my health for a long time now. Yet every time I go to commit to doing a talk somewhere or running a workshop or launching my group program, my mind says, 'Yeah, but what if your health fails you?' And I'm like, wow, that's still showing up. Well, okay, that can show up, but I'm not going to let the fear attached to that belief make the decisions for me. I know now that I can take good care of myself and do my best to resource myself with what I need for different situations.

Now I invite you to rewrite the words, phrases and thoughts that you previously wrote down. Looking at the list you've got, I want you to write down something from the perspective of your wise, strong, courageous, caring, compassionate self. This can be tricky, so I want you to notice what shows up while you write down the new words, phrases and thoughts. You might feel some resistance or notice that your sneaky self-critic is getting louder. See if you can notice whatever you're experiencing and still do the exercise. You might find it helpful to say them out loud to yourself, or you might just want to say them quietly to yourself and notice how it feels when you say these from this different perspective. Look at your first list and do your best to respond in a more compassionate way. You might like to make some notes of what you noticed.

Here are a couple of examples to help get you started:

What if I can't get it done in time?

*New response:* I can plan for the time I need and ask for realistic time frames before agreeing to do something.

I don't know how to do (x). I'm going to look foolish, and I'll be criticised. All my peers are going to think I'm useless.

*New response:* I can ask for help where I need to. Most people tend to be helpful and understanding. I don't have to know everything.

When you have done this, allow yourself some time to reflect on how that felt, how easy or challenging it was to shift your perspective, and what you noticed when you were trying to talk to yourself or encourage yourself in a different way.

Before we close out this chapter …

## Let's play a game

I'm probably showing my age, which I'm fine with because as I age, I believe more and more that with age comes wisdom. At least, that's what I'm telling myself. Plus, not everyone has the privilege of aging, so let's do our best to embrace it.

There used to be an improv show called *Whose Line Is It Anyway?* I really enjoyed watching it and thought the actors were so talented. They would be given a particular topic or word, and then they would riff off one another and develop stories out of pretty much nothing or very little. I think life is rather like that. We kind of riff off one another and make a life up as we go along. No one has an instruction manual or a map of how it's meant to look. We just get on and do our best under the circumstances we are in, with the knowledge, skills and resources that we have at the time. Like the improv show, we are also heavily influenced by the people who come before us and the people we interact with. From a very young age, we take our lead from the adults in our lives, often without the ability to question things we are told about ourselves or the world. Depending on the environment we were born into, this information can be helpful or harmful. As Professor Paul Gilbert says, if we were taken at birth and raised by different people, or even just born into different families in different places, we would not be the version of ourselves that we are. We are socially constructed beings, and we can't discount our own experiences when we look at who we are and how we engage in the world and with ourselves.

Take a moment to look back at your previous reflections on your word cage and pick out any beliefs or stories you have about yourself or self-care, e.g. 'I can't do xyz', 'Resting is lazy', 'I should be able to do xyz' or 'If I focus on myself, I'll become self-centred.' Create three columns (or use the table below) and write the belief in the first column and then think about where this belief came from and put that in the second column. Is this really what you believe, or is this an old message or story that has been passed to you by someone else? Finally, think about whether this belief is helpful to you or if it's something that gets in the way of you treating yourself well and living the life you want. Add this to the final column.

As you do this exercise, remember to go gently with yourself. For many of us, looking back over past experiences can be challenging and painful. Only engage to the level that you feel comfortable with right now, knowing you can return to these exercises at any time. You might also choose to work on some of these with a supportive other, perhaps a trusted friend, a coach or therapist.

| Belief/Story I tell Myself | Whose thought is it anyway? | Is this helpful or harmful? |
|---|---|---|
| | | |
| | | |
| | | |
| | | |
| | | |

Now think about which of these beliefs you want to carry forward with you and which you'd like to leave behind. You can continue to use these questions when different beliefs and stories show up as you go about your life.

One last thing before we move on. I invite you to write down the limiting beliefs that stand out the most for you. I call these your *red-flag beliefs*. These are the ones that tend to be the most pervasive and sticky. You know, the really familiar ones that have been around a long time and show up all over the place.

Your personal red-flag beliefs:

_____
_____
_____
_____
_____

Now you're aware of your red flag beliefs, you'll be able to spot them more easily when you start to think about the possibilities for your future and how you would like life to be different. We don't want those limiting beliefs or your sneaky self-critic in the driving seat anymore.

## MAKING SENSE OF FEELINGS AND THE BELIEFS THAT HOLD YOU BACK

### *Maria's Case Study*

*I didn't realise I was neglecting myself until my body gave me no other option. It crept in slowly, so slowly I almost missed it. It started around the time an extended family member was facing significant health issues. That's when I unknowingly began to feel the responsibility of her illness like it was my own. I didn't stop to think about the emotional weight I was carrying; I just kept going.*

*Within a couple of months, I felt an exhaustion I couldn't shake. I thought I had sinusitis. There were odd pressures in my head, headaches that kept returning and a rising tide of anxiety I hadn't felt in over a decade. I was supposed to be celebrating my husband's sixtieth birthday and going on a family trip, but I didn't want to go. Well, I wanted to go, but I didn't feel like I could.*

*My anxiety felt so severe I didn't know what to do. I remember waking my husband one morning and saying, 'Don't go to work. I need you here.' That wasn't like me, but I couldn't keep pretending everything was fine. Together, we went through my to-do list that morning to try to ease my anxiety and overwhelm. It helped a little, enough to get me ready to go on our family trip. But I wasn't well. I couldn't sleep. I had no peace. I was still powering through for everyone else.*

*Over the Christmas holidays, I left a family gathering early, which was unlike me. I remember my mum's shocked response when I told her I was going. I came home and cried. Not because of a single moment, but because I felt entirely undone. A build-up of stress and tears waiting to be shed. With yet another blinding headache, I called the out-of-hours Healthline. Over the next few weeks, I saw doctors, took tablets and chased answers. My body was screaming for the attention I hadn't given it in years.*

*Eventually, my GP sat me down and said, 'I think you're depressed.' Those words landed hard and brought with them more tears. But deep down, I didn't think I was depressed. I felt completely and utterly burnt out. Numb. I felt like I had no headspace left to live my own life because I was carrying too much of everyone else's. I felt like I was living their lives instead of mine.*

*At first, I thought I just needed a break. So, I cancelled everything for the next month, all social plans gone. I gave myself space, and I still didn't feel well. I went back to the doctor and saw a specialist, only to be told I was physically fine. What I was feeling was most likely pressure I was creating inside my head. It clicked. I'd spent a lifetime putting everyone else first. Saying yes, being the dependable one, it had finally caught up with me.*

*There was a moment I'll never forget. A paramedic knocked on my door and asked me if I could take my elderly neighbour to the hospital. I'd just brought my elderly mum home for dinner, so I told them there was no way I could take her and asked them to apologise on my behalf. For the first time, I said no, and then I sobbed, feeling guilt-ridden. I wasn't used to choosing myself, but I knew I had to. I had to let go of old patterns. I had to start saying no to other people in my life, even when it hurt, even when guilt screamed inside me. What's painful now is realising that so many of the people I gave to so freely never gave back. It was a one-way street. I don't regret caring, but I do regret not caring for myself too.*

*It brings up a lot of emotion to look back and think about all the ways I neglected myself. On reflection, I realise I had been neglecting my own needs for decades. I just wasn't present in my own life. I never stopped to ask myself what I wanted; I was too busy saying yes to others and feeling responsible for everyone else's emotions. I'm only just now treating myself to nice things, like going shopping to choose clothes that I like, thinking about the foods I enjoy, or taking time to massage moisturiser into my body. I'm trying to appreciate all aspects of myself. Sadly, my marriage, my relationship with myself, and even time with my own family were neglected. It's still hard to say that, but it's the truth.*

*My recovery hasn't been quick. It took nine months, a rebirth of sorts, the birthing of a new version of myself. I'm getting stronger. I still wobble. But I'm learning to recognise what burnout feels like in my body. The worst part of this whole experience is realising what I'd done to myself and the self-blame that accompanies that. I'm shocked at how far I let it go. But the best part is knowing I can choose differently now. Now I press pause and ask myself, 'Do I want to do this?' If the answer's no, I don't do it. It's powerful, realising I'm allowed to pause. It's okay for me to say no. I'm allowed to be here for myself, not just everyone else.*

*I used to feel full of stress, anxiety and guilt, but from now on, I'm choosing peace over obligation and joy over guilt. I'm making life choices for myself now.*

# *Congratulations, you finished Part I*

## Take a moment to CARE for yourself

**CELEBRATE**

Don't forget to celebrate along the way. Even small moments of celebration can make a difference to how you feel.

What is one thing you are proud of yourself for?

How will you celebrate? Be specific about what you'll do and when. You're more likely to do it if you're specific.

Remember, celebrations don't have to be big or elaborate. It's the act of slowing down, acknowledging and celebrating that matters, not what it looks like.

**APPRECIATE**

Appreciate where you are at right now.

What is something you are grateful for?

What is something you need to do your best to accept right now?

**REFLECT**

What is something you would like to change?

**EXHALE**

Take a moment to do ten soothing breaths.

*Be the star in the show you want to attend, rather than a character in someone else's play.*

*May your show have a storyline full of wonder, splendour, love, passion and compassion for yourself and others.*

# PART II
# EXPLORE THE POSSIBILITIES

# 4

# *What Happened to Your Dreams?*

My life changed when I started to pay attention to myself and ask different questions. One of the questions I asked was: *What happened to your dreams, Hayley?*

I want to ask you the same question.

\*\*\*

For far too long, women have lived under a false narrative; one that tells us that we can only do so much, whilst at the same time expecting us to be able to do it all – be superwoman. Both can't be true; we've been sold a lie. It's one that can leave us feeling inadequate and full of self-doubt.

> *Self-doubt is like a weight that drags you down*
> *as you try to swim forward in the sea of your dreams.*

You have an idea and a part of you knows that it's brilliant. But wait, you're not meant to be brilliant, and you're certainly not meant to tell people you're brilliant or even suggest that you might be. Don't brag, don't 'big note' yourself, don't get 'too big for your boots'. We've heard them all. As a woman, it's much preferred if you are quiet and calm and available for others so they can be brilliant. But what if that's not the only way to be? What if you can claim your brilliance and allow it to emerge into the light in whatever form it is meant to take? What if you could choose to live life on your terms, in a way that suited you as the individual you are?

Often, the first stumbling block is being unsure about what you like, what you're good at or how you want your life to look. This can be because you've never allowed yourself the time to get to know yourself, or because you've always seen yourself through the lens of other people. Perhaps people who would not be served by you knowing who you are or how brilliant you really are.

The socialisation of women across centuries has been so very different to that of men, and it has created barriers, both visible and unseen. Barriers that prevent far too many women from living a fulfilling, exciting and authentic life. Barriers that may have prevented you from living out your dreams. It's time for that to change.

Who was it? Who told you to stop dreaming? For me, it started in classrooms: 'Stop daydreaming', 'Pay attention', 'You're not here to look out of the window'. Maybe this was your experience too. I then had dreams of being on stage or in films. I loved putting on a play, drawing on my imagination and playing my own adventures in my mind. My dad discouraged my dreams of acting. He told me I'd have to be very good to get anywhere in the industry. I now believe this was coming from a place of protection. He worked in television, and no doubt saw how women were treated and didn't want that for his daughter. Unfortunately, the message landed with me as 'you're not good enough and should think of something else'. I then decided that journalism would be a good choice, as I had loved writing from an early age. My favourite subject was English and I loved writing stories and poetry. Again, my dad told me how hard the industry was, and I'd have to be very good to succeed.

More words cut into me, telling me I wasn't good enough. How I longed for him to tell me how smart I was, how creative I was and how if I worked hard, I could do any of those things I dreamed of. He suggested I attend secretarial college to learn typing and shorthand that would secure me good employment for my lifetime. I convinced myself at such an early age that I couldn't have the life I wanted. It's no wonder I dropped out of school early. What was the point of suffering in a system that felt so awful if I couldn't do what I wanted at the end? I did end up training as a secretary, and it did provide me with employment, but never satisfaction. In my mid-twenties, I decided a big change was what I wanted. A family friend told me I would love Australia, so I made the choice to leave the UK and see what Australia had to offer. It wasn't all smooth sailing, as I mentioned earlier, but I took risks, made changes, learnt more about myself and the things I enjoyed, started to dream, studied and became a clinical psychologist. With a career that spanned almost two decades, I went on to create a business and life that I love.

> *Who knew daydreams could come true! Never stop dreaming.*

This is possible for you too.
    What dreams have you let go of?

*You can live with regret or
you can offer yourself compassion
and remember that you have been
doing the best you can
in the circumstances you are in
with the skills and knowledge that you have*

## Current Self and aspirations

Just because we've let go of some dreams doesn't mean we can't pick them back up or dream new dreams. We have a mind that is capable of endless imagining. This is where we get to slow down and dream for a while. We all have dreams. The problem is that life often gets too busy and dreams can get pushed out to the side and forgotten. They end up in the dream corner collecting dust.

Perhaps you've been telling yourself that your dreams aren't achievable, or you don't deserve them, or dreams are for dreamers and you're all about the practical real-life stuff. Well, I'm here to tell you that your dreams are valid and it's okay for you to explore them more and see what you'd like to act on. Think about all the things you long for, the opportunities you wish would come your way, the places you'd love to go, the bold steps you've been wanting to take in your life but never quite manage to. Whatever your dreams and aspirations are, they don't have to make sense right now, and you don't need to have the solution for how you're going to achieve them. Right now, you just get to dream and allow your imagination to play and create.

Let's start with how you feel about yourself and your life as it is. Think about what you are doing and whether these are your choices or being done through a sense of obligation or habit. Consider whether you're living a life that feels aligned or one that fits a way of being that you think is expected of you.

What three words would you use to describe your life and how you currently feel? Write them down and then think about how you feel when you read them. Would you like things to be different?

Rather than staying stuck to some rigid rules you've picked up somewhere along the way, try allowing some spaciousness into your days and see what emerges in terms of what you might like to be doing. Gift yourself some time, whether it's a few minutes, a few hours, or a day to explore and delight in what life could be like for you. Try your best not to limit yourself and be curious about what shows up. Your tricky mind is highly likely going to step in and make judgements and be practical and all those other dream-destroying things your mind can do. When this happens, do your best to return your attention to your dreams. You might want to acknowledge that your mind is just trying to keep you safe from making any hasty or bad decisions. Remind yourself that this is just a time for dreaming. Even if something seems impossible or completely out of character for you, that's totally okay. Dream away, darling.

## Pause

Take a moment to write down some of the things you'd love to do. Don't overthink it; just allow yourself to dream, be curious, be playful.

Now you've written down some of your dreams and desires, notice how you feel. Do you feel different in your body? Do you have a sense of excitement, joy, fear or self-doubt? Whatever it is that you're feeling, just do your best to notice it and allow your experience to be whatever it is.

In the next chapter, we're going to explore values and how we can use these to design the life we want.

*What if you listened to your own wisdom
and took action based on your own choices,
rather than doing what you think
others want you to do?*

# 5

## *What Matters Most to You?*

Values are like signposts; they act as guiding principles in your life. They relate to what is important and meaningful for you as an individual. There are no right or wrong values, just different values. We can think of them like pizza. You might choose deep-dish Hawaiian, and I'd choose a thin-crust veggie pizza without cheese. Neither of these are right nor wrong. They're just different. Although we could start a whole debate about whether to put pineapple on a pizza. You share similar values with some of the people in your life and are likely to have some differing values too. I imagine if your values are extremely different from some of the people in your life, you might notice discomfort and tension when these values clash. Perhaps you find these relationships more challenging.

Your values can help guide your decision-making, behaviours and interactions with the people around you. You may have learnt many of your values in your earlier years from your family, culture, communities you've been a part of and society in general. If you haven't spent any time reflecting on your values, when you do, you may realise that some of these values don't fit with how you now think, feel and behave as an adult. You might want to replace them with values that feel more aligned for you. As you go through this process, over time, you might notice your values shift, or you'll reconnect with values you hold but haven't been living in alignment with. Before you start criticising yourself, remember, none of us are living in line with our values all of the time. This is a prime opportunity for your self-critic to show up and remind you how you're not living in alignment with some of your values.

Would we all like to be living in complete alignment with our values? Yes, I'm sure we would. Is that possible? Heck no!

None of us are perfect human beings.

First, remember you're a human with a tricky mind. Behaviour change and complete consistency is h. a. r. d. for all of us. Second, you are going to have times in your life where you encounter values conflicts, and you'll have to decide which value is the most important to you in that circumstance. This means you'll be out of alignment with another or several other values. Even when you are strongly in alignment with a value in a particular domain of your life, that's unlikely to be all the time. It's okay; you're not aiming for perfection in any of this. Your values are just signposts to let you know what path you want to be on and help redirect you when you're heading in a different direction.

When you figure out what your values are, this gives you information. You can reflect on what you value and what is important and meaningful to you. You can then go on to create a life that honours those values and doesn't have you feeling like everything is hard work and stressful. You might discover that you want to make some important changes. You may realise that you don't have to change everything because some of it already aligns with who you want to be and how you want to live. I have no doubt your relationships, health, work and other domains are important to you. Your life matters, so let's get you designing it in a way that honours how much your overall wellbeing matters too. Knowing your values can also assist you when you want to implement boundaries with someone or in a particular context. We'll talk more about boundaries in a later chapter.

You'll notice the questions in this section are broken down into segments. You can put just a few words to summarise those key values in the different domains. You may find that a lot of your values cross over different domains in your life. Again, this isn't an invitation for your self-critic to jump in and start giving you a hard time. As I said earlier, none of us are living completely in line with our values, and certainly not all the time. So, be gentle with yourself during an exercise like this. When you give yourself time to sit and reflect, sometimes it's what doesn't go on the list that stands out to you. There might be things that you spend so much time doing when really, you'd rather be using your time and energy for something else. You might also notice that your mind wants to put everything as a priority, but you know that they can't all take top priority. Your priorities change on different days, in different seasons and in different contexts, and that's okay. It's more than okay; it's expected and necessary.

## *Pause*

Take some time to reflect on your values. Check in with yourself first and engage to the level that feels right for you in this moment.

Allow yourself plenty of time for this exercise. Try not to rush it. If you can't complete it in one sitting, that's totally fine. Do a little bit and come back to it again later. Also, if any of the questions are written in a way that doesn't quite make sense for you, just rewrite them and ask yourself in a way that allows you to access the information that is helpful for you.

Your values sit across different domains in your life. Sometimes they are the same and sometimes they are different depending on the domain you're thinking about. This section sets out some different domains and asks questions relating to that. Don't worry if you are repeating yourself across domains. It just means you have a strong value that fits many areas of your life.

**Relationship – intimate and friendships**

- What personal qualities would I like to bring to my relationships?
- What types of relationships would I like to build?
- What level of intimacy is important to me?
- How would I interact with others if I were the ideal version of myself in these relationships?

**Personal development and learning**

- What do I value about learning, education, training and/or personal growth?
- What new skills would I like to learn?
- What knowledge would I like to gain?
- What further education (if any) appeals to me?
- What sort of student would I like to be?
- What personal qualities would I like to apply to this area of my life?

**Caregiving** – Caregiving might be of children, parents, spouse, relatives, clients, fur babies (animals) or whatever caregiving means for you.

- What sort of caregiver would I like to be?
- What sort of qualities would I like to have?
- What sort of relationships would I like to build with who I'm caring for?
- How would I behave if I were the 'ideal' version of myself?

### Business/work

- What do I value in my business/work?
- What would make it feel more meaningful?
- What kind of business owner/worker would I like to be?
- If I were living up to my own 'ideal' standards, what personal qualities would I like to bring to my work?
- What sort of work relationships would I like to nurture?

### Recreation

- What sorts of hobbies, sports or leisure activities do I enjoy?
- How do I relax and unwind?
- How do I have fun?
- What sorts of activities would I like to do?

### Health, physical and mental wellbeing

- What is important to me in relation to maintaining my health (physical and mental wellbeing)?
- How do I want to look after my health with regard to sleep, nutrition, exercise, nervous system regulation, smoking, alcohol, illicit drugs, etc.?
- Why is this important to me?

### Community

- How would I like to contribute to my community or environment, e.g. through volunteering, recycling, or supporting a group/charity/political party?
- What sort of environments would I like to create at home and at work?
- What environments would I like to spend more time in?

### Culture

- What traditions or customs are important to me?
- What else would I like to learn about my culture?
- How would I like to express my culture in my everyday life?
- How important is it to me to understand different cultural perspectives?

**Spirituality** – Whatever spirituality means to you is what matters here. It may be as simple as communing with nature, or as formal as participation in an organised religious setting.

- What does spirituality mean to me?
- What is important to me in relation to my spirituality?
- How do I want to connect with my spirituality?

Now you've done that, you can take some time to rate your values. Write down a few key words to summarise your values for each domain. Once you have written them down, rate them between 0 (low importance) to 10 (high importance) in terms of *importance*. You can have several values that score the same number.

Next, you can rate them in terms of *alignment*. Rate how closely you are living in alignment to each value between 0 (not at all aligned) to 10 (very aligned with my value). Again, you can have several values that score the same number. Remember, this isn't an exercise designed for your self-critic to jump in and start giving you a hard time, but that sneaky little sucker might try. Please be gentle with yourself during this exercise.

Next, rank your values in order of the *priority* you place on working on them right now, with 10 as the highest ranking, then 9 the next highest, and so on. There are no right or wrong answers to this. It doesn't matter what your friend/partner/family/colleague's values or ranking of values are. This is only about what is important to you.

Once you have all this information, you might want to start making some changes so you feel more in alignment with your values. You certainly don't need to be doing that in every domain straight away, nor would I recommend that. Some areas of your life may feel more important to you than others. Start with maybe one or two areas for change so you don't feel overwhelmed before you even start. What do you see as your top three values? Remember, these can change over time, but it can be helpful to be aware of what your current top values are when it comes to making decisions and new choices. You might like to write these down.

Now you've explored and connected with your values from your current self perspective, let's go and think about your future, what you might want and any wisdom your future self might have for you.

*If your heart could set sail and compassion
could be your sea breeze,
where would you like to go?*

# 6

# *Connecting to the Wisdom of Your Future Self*

One of the things I do on a regular basis is connect with my future self. The first time I did this, I was surprised at how difficult I found it, but as I practised, I learnt that there was so much inner wisdom and comfort I was able to connect with. It really became a profound practice for me and one that I'm so grateful for. Like with any new practice, go gently with yourself. Do your best to allow your experience to be whatever it is without trying to control it too much, even though that's likely what your mind is going to want to do. This really is just about allowing yourself to be curious and open to possibilities.

In a moment, I'm going to invite you to take some time to imagine your ideal life. What you'd be doing, what your everyday would look like, and what your work would be like. This is an opportunity to allow yourself to dream. Try not to make judgements and don't be surprised if that's exactly what your mind starts to do. Your mind is very likely going to come in and start saying things like: 'Yeah, but you can't do that', 'Well, that's not realistic', 'Who do you think you are to want that?' or 'You should be grateful for what you already have.' Try your best not to concern yourself with those thoughts in this moment, just brainstorm. Whenever your mind starts with the judgement, come back to the question – if this was my absolute ideal life, what would it look like?

I say 'try not to concern yourself' because, even if it's not something that you can do in the exact form you're thinking, it's going to give you clues about what's important to you. Then you can look at it and adapt it to something that is realistic and achievable for you in this current season of your life.

For example, you might have your own business and dream of running it from a beachside destination like Bali. You've seen other people doing it, so you know it's possible, but perhaps this wouldn't fit with your type of business or current season of life. You could think about what it is about that you might enjoy and come up with ways to bring some of those aspects into your current circumstances. Maybe you could get outside more and be in the sunshine and fresh air. You could choose to take more time out and visit the beach, park or favourite location with your family. You wouldn't be there all the time, but you'll have brought more of what you want into your life. Perhaps you could go and work in your favourite café. Maybe you can't do all your work in a different setting, but maybe you could do your accounting or admin there. Imagine how much more fun it could be doing your admin in a café, drinking something nice, rather than sitting in an office. I love working in cafés, but I stopped doing it as much when I started living at the beach. I can see the ocean from my window, something I'm extremely grateful for and never thought would be a part of my future. The view tends to keep me working from home, but writing this is prompting me to get out to cafés more as I remember how much I enjoy it. Maybe as you're reading this, I'll be sitting in a café somewhere doing my work. At times, we can get caught in all or nothing thinking. If we shift that perspective, we can create a life that is full of experiences and activities we enjoy.

Let's take some time to brainstorm. Let your imagination run wild. 'In an ideal world', what would you be doing and what would life and work/business be like? How do you want to feel? Remember to add in things you enjoy. Maybe you'd like to take more regular breaks, or go on road trips, or be able to go to a particular type of event or appointment during certain days. Once you've got all that written down, you can start to think about how you could plan your life to factor those in. Don't just think about how work would look, but also what you want your life to look like so that you can create it in a way that fits with how you want it to be, not how you've been told it should be. This can feel challenging at first, particularly given the patriarchal, capitalist system we live within.

There are no right or wrong answers here. This is different for all of us based on our dreams, desires and values, and that's totally okay. In fact, that is what makes life such an interesting tapestry. Imagine if we all wanted the same things and created our lives to be identical to one another. Yawn, how boring that would be.

This brainstorming exercise will help you gain further clarity for when you want to set some new goals for yourself. You might desire more time to be creative or to spend with your children or loved ones. Maybe you want more time in nature or to watch your favourite shows. You might want time to learn another language or the opportunity for long and leisurely naps. Maybe it's travel, dancing, starting a new business or setting yourself a challenge to overcome. Only you know what you really desire, and even then, it might still be deep inside you waiting to come out.

## CONNECTING TO THE WISDOM OF YOUR FUTURE SELF

There is a power in writing these down. It allows you to see what you really want and can act as a starting point to making the changes you desire. It also gives you a record that you can look back on and see where you're at in relation to where you want to be. I've had women I work with say to me, 'That was my dream, and now I'm living it/part of it.' It's so beautiful when that happens. It's so powerful because it then acts as a motivator to continue to create a life of your choosing. You give yourself experiences to look back on that remind you that you can do the things you want to do.

## *Pause*

Take some time now to brainstorm. I've given you some prompts to get you started. Remember, check in with yourself first and engage to the level that feels right for you in this moment.

- If I could design my life in a way I really want, what would it look and feel like?
- What would I be doing for work (or would I be working)?
- Where would I live?
- Who would I spend time with?
- What activities would I engage in?
- What would I stop doing?
- What would I start doing?

Now you've thought about your ideal life, it's time for a guided meditation to help you connect with your future self and hear any wisdom they want to share. You might like to record yourself reading this so you can then close your eyes and play it back, or you can use the QR code, and I will guide you. At the end of this script are some questions. You can use these as prompts to help you reflect after the meditation.

### CONNECTING TO FUTURE SELF

*I invite you to find a comfortable position, ideally in an upright position with your feet flat on the floor and an open diaphragm. You can open your diaphragm by gently lifting your shoulders up and back. Most important is that you listen to what your body needs and give yourself permission to do that. You might be sitting on a chair or the floor, laying down on the floor or your bed, or in any other position that suits you.*

*I will be inviting you to imagine different things, and for some people imagining looks different. It doesn't matter whether you bring to mind complete images, partial images or even just a felt sense of what I am describing. Take a moment to give yourself permission to experience this in whatever way your experience unfolds and know that at any time you can choose to come out of this practice and return to it as you desire.*

*If you feel comfortable, gently close your eyes or rest your gaze in front of you. Gently bring your attention to your breath and allow your breath to find its own soothing rhythm of in- and out-breaths. Each out-breath allowing you to become more relaxed and comfortable. Any outside sounds can just be noticed as you leave the noise and stress of the outside world and focus on the soothing rhythm of your breath here in this present moment.*

*I invite you to picture yourself standing before a peaceful body of water. Imagine dropping a pebble into the water. Notice how the ripples spread out and eventually settle, allowing the water to become still and peaceful again. Notice how you feel this stillness and peace within you. As you look to your left, you notice a path surrounded by trees and flowers. Now imagine yourself walking along the path. As you walk further along the path, you feel even more peaceful. As you wander further down the path, you notice an archway of beautiful flowers, and as you walk under the archway, you find yourself in a different place. You are now five years in the future. Allow yourself to look around and notice what you see. Are you still in nature? Are there buildings? Just take a moment to notice the details of where you are. This is where your future self lives, five years from now.*

*As you're taking in your surroundings, notice there's someone slowly coming towards you. You can sense they are friendly. As they approach, you notice this person is you, a little older. This is your future self. Take a moment to greet your future self and notice how your future self greets you back, welcoming you into this time and place five years from now.*

*What does your future self look like? Notice how they stand, how they look at you, what they are wearing. Really try to get a sense of the essence of your future self.*

*Now move with your future self to a place where you can sit together and have a conversation. Perhaps there's a bench or a comfy chair or a soft patch of grass or sand.*

*Begin by asking your future self:*

*'What are you doing with your life now?'*
*'What do you love about your life?'*

*Take a moment to listen to the answers.*
*Now ask your future self the following questions:*

*'What do I need to know to get me from where I am now to where you are?'*
*'What would be most helpful?'*

*Listen to what your future self is telling you.*
*Now tell your future self one thing that is currently bothering, worrying or challenging you and ask, 'How did you overcome this challenge?'*

*Next, ask, 'What is one thing you'd like me to know?'*

*Finally, ask your future self to tell you one word that is important for you to remember when you're feeling stressed or need support to keep going towards your goals. What is that one word? Do your best to remember it, but don't put pressure on yourself. Trust that if you don't remember, it doesn't matter; you'll remember it if you need to.*

*As you are about to leave, you notice that your future self has a gift for you. Receive the gift. What is it? What do you notice about it? Ask them, 'What would you like me to know about this gift?'*

*Bringing this visit to a close, thank your future self for being here with you today and sharing so much wisdom. Now, take a deep breath, breathing in this experience, remembering what you need to remember. It's okay if you don't remember everything; you can revisit your future self at another time. Trust that you will remember what you are meant to remember for now.*

*Now, as you look to your right, you see the flowered archway. Go back through and follow the path back to the peaceful body of water and the present time.*

*Now as you leave the water, you travel back to where you are, noticing the landscape, the skyline and the familiar places. Finally, you come back to the environment you are in.*

*In a few moments, I'm going to invite you to open your eyes and remain silent. I'll prompt you to open your notebook and write down the things you want to remember about this experience with your future self.*

*Take a few more slow, soothing breaths, just noticing your in-breath and out-breath. Now start to notice the sounds around you. Gently guide your attention to how it feels to be sitting or lying where you are. Gently make some small movements with your fingers and toes. As you feel ready, you can open your eyes and bring your attention back to the place you are in and stretch your body or give your body whatever it needs right now. Remain quiet and start your reflective writing. I've given you some prompts to help you.*

*How did I feel in this meditation?*
*What arose for me?*
*What did my future self want me to know?*
*What word did my future self share with me?*
*What was the gift my future self gave me?*
*What does that mean to me now?*
*What would I like to say to my future self?*

Now you've got some clarity on your values, brainstormed some ideas for your ideal life and met with your future self, let's think about what a successful life would look like for you.

## Success is a story you can write for yourself

In all the work I do with others, I come from a place of there is no 'one right way' to do something. You need to know yourself well. You must change the relationship you have with yourself and honour who you are, the season you're in, your values and the capabilities, strengths and challenges you have. This looks similar in some ways for all of us, and very different in other ways. That has got to be okay, because otherwise you are trying to live by someone else's rules, and trying to live someone else's life. That would be like going to a stranger's wardrobe, picking out an outfit and expecting it to fit you and your style perfectly.

You don't just want to take scripts from other people saying, 'You need to do it this way or that way.' If you do, you can end up feeling like there's something wrong with you if you don't get the results they're promoting. You can feel defective or incapable, that somehow you're not enough, and that's not okay. It's not okay at all. You need to do it your own way, and that can be difficult. But it absolutely is possible. I know this because many years ago I lived my life like a chameleon. I did what I needed to do to fit with what people needed me to be, how they wanted me to be and what I thought I should be. I aimed for what I thought success 'should' be. I absolutely don't do that anymore. So, I know with insight, reflection, willingness and support it can be done. In the next section, I'll help you to reflect on what you think needs to change and how you can learn to do things differently. But before we move on, let's define what success means to you.

In today's modern and competitive world, we are led to believe that if we look, work, achieve and be a certain way, we will be happy and loved. We live in a society that constantly gives us messages about success, what it is and how to achieve it. But how often do you stop and check in with yourself about whether those versions of success are meaningful or important to you? For me, success looks like having enough time to take care of my wellbeing and not feeling rushed when I start my day. I'm no longer in my active parenting stage so it's easier for me to go slower nowadays. Success for me means having the autonomy and flexibility to be able to put things aside if my son, husband or cherished friends need support. Ultimately though, success for me is the caring, loving, supportive relationship I now have with myself. After years of self-doubt, self-criticism, self-hatred and self-neglect, I now have a relationship with myself that I cherish. I have cultivated a part of myself that is so compassionate. This part of me is my closest companion, fondest friend, greatest cheerleader and wisest guide. This connection and renewed relationship with myself has enabled me to create a life that allows me to thrive.

I want you to have that too, because I know how different life feels when you honour yourself and your wellbeing. You stop speaking to yourself in a way that minimises, invalidates and shames you. You move from self-neglect, and continually treating your needs like they don't matter, to a relationship that is understanding, accepting, caring and compassionate.

I invite you to pause and think about the things that have felt important and meaningful to you, why you chose and started them, and also some of the things that you might want or need. There are no right and wrong answers here. If you're not sure, just let your mind wander and see what answers show up. Be as open and curious as you can.

## *Pause*

Take some time to reflect. I've included some questions to help you. Remember to check in with yourself and engage to the level that feels right for you in the moment.

What feels most important and meaningful to you about your life? This might be particular interests you have, family, friends, your work or business, anything that matters to you.

- *Why did I choose this in the first place?*
- *What are some of the reasons I do what I do?*

Think about what you'd like for yourself, in any domain of your life. You might want to write these separately or just as an overall picture of how you'd like things to be.

- *What is something I keep thinking about?*
- *What have I been excited about but then not done?*

## CONNECTING TO THE WISDOM OF YOUR FUTURE SELF

- *What is something I find myself frequently talking or dreaming about?*

You might also like to think about the following:

- *How much money do I need to support my household budget/lifestyle?*
- *Ideally, how much do I want to work?*
- *What type of work do I want to do?*
- *What types of carer roles am I willing to engage in?*

If you run your own business, you could ask yourself:

- *What client group do I want to work with?*
- *How many clients do I want to see in a day or a week?*
- *How many hours do I want to work in a day or a week?*
- *What products or services do I want to offer?*
- *What could help make my work more manageable?*

If we were speaking three, six or twelve months from now and you felt like your life was more successful, in whatever way is meaningful to you, what would you be telling me about? Choose one of these timeframes, or all three; it's up to you.

If you didn't manage to answer all the questions, that's okay. You might have answered enough for your requirements, or you may choose to come back later and answer some more.

It can be helpful to have something to refer back to as a reminder of your hopes and desires. Some people like to have these somewhere visible. If you do this, be aware that after a while your brain will stop seeing them – yes, this is a thing. Your brain will adapt and you'll stop noticing them, so it can be helpful to move them every now and again. That gives your brain novelty, and you'll pay attention to them again. Told you that you have a tricky brain.

In my former work as a clinical psychologist and my current work as a coach, I have found asking questions that encourage curiosity and deeper thinking have been so impactful, together with holding space for the person to do the reflections. Whilst I'm not with you in person, I hope the opportunities for reflection so far have been impactful for you and that together we have created a space where you feel held.

The other piece to bringing about change is to learn to do things differently. As the saying goes, if you keep doing what you're doing, you'll keep getting what you're getting. Basically, if nothing changes, then nothing can change. You have to look at the things you'll need to do differently so you're not repeating old patterns or sabotaging your own success. I made the choice many years ago to learn to do it differently. I worked hard to change the relationship I have with myself, and I am so glad that I did. It really has been life-changing. It has had a positive impact on all areas of my life, and I can honestly say I'm a nicer person to be around because of it. If you're ready to acknowledge that it's not your fault but it is your responsibility, keep reading. We're going to do some new learning in the next chapters. I'll be here with you along the way, and I know you've got this.

### Rebecca's case study

I'm only now coming to understand the self-abandonment and the self-neglect. For me, it was normalised. Having a need, taking up space, and owning desire were so foreign to me. That's what other people did. My job was to enable them to meet those needs and to fulfil those desires. It was perpetual self-abandonment and self-neglect. I had no idea what my own needs were. It wasn't even a conscious choice; it was the water I swam in. I'd been raised to believe that taking up space or having a need was somehow selfish or unnecessary. So, I learnt to disappear. I showed up for everyone else, and I disappeared from myself.

The change point wasn't just one moment, but a series of brave decisions. At sixteen, I thought I had my career all mapped out. But on the very first day of my clinical placement at university, I knew it wasn't right. That realisation was terrifying and liberating. It gave me permission to rewrite my story. I moved cities, I pursued multiple graduate programs and I began to reinvent. The changes were uncomfortable and confusing, but they cracked something open in me.

Then, at the edge of a life I thought I wanted, I had another moment of truth. I was engaged to be married and driving on a highway one day when I realised neither of us truly wanted the other. We wanted the versions we hoped each other would become. So, I gave back the ring, cancelled the registry, disappointed a great many people and came home with my tail between my legs. I must have had a deep knowing in that moment that I was worthy of making a different choice. I didn't know what I was choosing. I just knew I was making a different choice.

Working in education, I advocated fiercely for my students and one day, it hit me: what if I offered myself the same compassion I gave to them? Having a major depressive episode and not being able to function was like a dissociation from this self that I was becoming. It was so wrenching. I didn't know how I would survive, but clawing my way back from that I knew I needed to do things differently. It meant leaving my job and establishing different relationships with friends and family.

I think the most significant tipping point for me has been exploring my neurodivergence, transitioning from working harder to understanding why things are hard. Once I knew my brain and nervous system were different, that I'm not failing, that I'm not bad or wrong, but just different, I remember it was like a wave of self-compassion washing over me. Understanding my neurodivergence has been an invitation to reflect and reimagine how I want to live, not just surviving but thriving authentically.

These days, I still fall into old patterns. I catch myself abandoning my own needs, especially when I'm in environments that echo past wounds. But the difference is I can see it now. I feel the resentment bubbling up, and I pause. What value did I just step over? What expectation did I buy into that wasn't mine to carry?

I try to meet these moments with grace, and to me, grace means accepting that I'm messy. It means acknowledging the hard without needing to fix it right away. It means letting go of perfection, of pressure, of the illusion that I need to prove my worth to anyone, including myself.

There are still times I feel guilt and frustration, but I no longer beat myself up for not doing it all, or for needing rest, or for saying no. I'm learning to see my limits not as failures but as signs of my humanity. I am a precious and limited resource, not because I'm broken, but because I'm whole.

*Self-compassion isn't a magic wand. It's a practice. It's a slow trickle that waters my soul. Sometimes it feels like just a drop here or there, but those drops all add up. Over time, they've created something nourishing, something resilient, something that gives me hope.*

*I think my most significant learning has been that I'm inherently worthy. Worthiness is not something you hustle for or something you earn; it's true and inherent to you no matter what you do, no matter how you show up. I still wrestle with this at times, but it has become a new underlying principle for me. If I show up and I'm messy, that's okay. If I'm emotional, that's okay, and I intellectually understand this, but I don't think I've fully connected to it emotionally yet. I can't wait to see what self-compassion looks like for me next year, five years from now and ten years from now. I can only hope that what feels aspirational feels more actualised and that the intellectual understanding of worthiness is a deep, primal knowing. But in the meantime, I have grace.*

# *Congratulations, you finished Part II*

## Take a moment to CARE for yourself

### CELEBRATE

Don't forget to celebrate along the way. Even small moments of celebration can make a difference to how we feel.

What is one thing you are proud of yourself for?

How will you celebrate? Be specific about what you'll do and when. You're more likely to do it if you're specific.

Remember, celebrations don't have to be big or elaborate. It's the act of slowing down, acknowledging and celebrating that matters, not what it looks like.

### APPRECIATE

Appreciate where you are at right now.

What is something you are grateful for?

What is something you need to do your best to accept right now?

### REFLECT

What is something you would like to change?

### EXHALE

Take a moment to do ten soothing breaths.

Things change and drop away. That doesn't
make them useless or a waste of time.
Things need to change to make room for
new growth. It is an integral part of life
and essential to its overall beauty.

This is true for both nature and for us.

Instead of picking out the parts of yourself and
your life you like and rejecting the rest,
try a more compassionate approach
to accept it all and move forward
focusing on what you want.

# PART III

# LEARN TO DO IT DIFFERENTLY; CHOOSE YOU

# 7

# *Permission to Put Yourself First*

There has been very strong messaging, especially for women, about how we are meant to be in the world. Some of this messaging is received from caregivers, friends, colleagues, and some is received from society in general. Who you are in terms of how you contribute to others, and the world, has always been held in high regard. The more productive you are, the more worthwhile you are seen to be. At least, that's what a lot of societal messaging has been.

Many of us end up wearing self-neglect as some kind of badge of honour. But what if productivity and servitude equalling worth isn't true? What if you are inherently worthwhile purely because you are here? A lot of us have internalised these strong messages about productivity and worth and turned them into our own beliefs, often without considering what that means. It's important to acknowledge that the world is shaped by a patriarchal, capitalist, ableist and white-centric viewpoint and it sneaks into all aspects of your

## FROM SELF-NEGLECT TO SELF-COMPASSION

life. How you view yourself, how you behave towards yourself and others, and what decisions you make in your life are influenced by the context you live in.

*You can choose to do things differently.*
*You can choose yourself first.*

Self-neglect doesn't stamp its feet, shout or scream. It doesn't even complain. It just sits quietly in the corner like a 'good girl'. That is until it gets to the point where it can't stay quiet anymore. It can't sit by watching you shrink, fade, feel less than, and be depleted by other people's needs. That's when it starts to gently nudge, and when you don't listen to that, it gets louder and louder. Self-neglect starts to shout, scream, and demand until you listen. This may look like increased irritability, a growing sense of dissatisfaction, unexplained aches and pains, frequent illness, fatigue, overwhelm, empathy fatigue or full-blown burnout. How long will you ignore the signs? Have you ever stopped to wonder why you see your needs as less than those of other people? And what does it take for you to give yourself permission to acknowledge yourself?

I invite you to give yourself that permission right now.

I'm all about empowering women and helping them find their voice, step into their power and create the lives that they want. Whether it be about work or in personal domains, it all leads to creating a life that is values-aligned and in integrity with who you are and what you want for yourself.

You might be realising that because of everything else that needs your attention, you've not been able to do the things that are important to you, and now you want to change that. You want to commit to taking care of yourself, and it's so important that you do because the cost of self-neglect is high. We have started talking more about burnout, which in many ways is great, but sadly a lot of the conversations still seem to normalise women feeling overwhelmed, exhausted and emotionally drained. It's not normal and it can be devastating. Burnout can take weeks, months or even years to recover. I don't want that for you.

When you are so out of alignment with yourself and the life you want, something must change. You need to stop minimising the problems that show up, and the distress you are ignoring, and look at how you can make changes so you can thrive. You deserve that. If you don't choose that for yourself, it's unlikely that anyone else will. No one is coming to do the work for you. No one is going to hand you your values-aligned life wrapped in a bow.

It's up to you to choose – so please choose you.

When the guilt of taking time for yourself appears, which I know it will, you must be willing to choose yourself again and again. I want you to show up, be brave and make the changes before you have no choice but to deal with the fallout from your ongoing self-neglect.

## Showing up for yourself is not always so easy

I often hear people say things like:

- 'This is just the way it has to be. It's always been like this.'
- 'Burnout is inevitable these days.'
- 'You have to hit rock bottom before you realise you can't do it like that anymore.'
- 'We're all going to burn out at some stage, better it happens sooner rather than later.'

- 'Burnout is like a badge of honour we get to show how hard we've been working.'
- 'If I take care of others first, people will know how much I care about them.'

How did we get to a point where this feels so acceptable? A little piece of my soul feels crushed when I hear people say these things, and then I notice the anger I feel. Anger at the systems we work within, anger at the normalisation of something that is far from 'normal'. Something that can be so devastating for your health, relationships, opportunities, finances and your sense of self-worth is almost accepted as some kind of rite of passage in life, particularly as a woman. It has to stop! It's time to stop accepting this. It's time to focus on wellbeing and burnout prevention rather than waiting for things to fall apart before we consider taking care of ourselves. Let's demand that things be different, that the expectations of us be different. Let's stop accepting the status quo and make a commitment to ourselves to do things differently, so we can take care of ourselves whilst creating a life that feels meaningful, exciting and fulfilling. Are you with me?

Please, let's stop normalising self-neglect and burnout.

It's time to choose you – a healthy, content, fulfilled you. It's time to choose to do things differently. While this may seem challenging, scary, even unattainable, I promise you it is possible. You can make the choice and learn to do it differently. You have so much wisdom within you and it's time to start listening to it.

I again acknowledge my own privilege and recognise that not everyone has access to the same resources I do or is able to make the same choices, but we do all have some choices. They might not be choices between options that are ideal in that moment, but it's still important for you to decide which is the best choice for right now. When you have access to more information, more confidence, more resources and better healthcare, or because you didn't like the outcome of the choice you made, you can make a different choice. It's okay to change your mind.

Another thing to be mindful of is if your identity is connected to a major role in your life. Whether that is as a business owner, professional, parent, or something else, you run the risk of other important areas of your life being overlooked. Take a moment to think about how you introduce yourself. Do you tend to list off your roles first? One of the reasons you can over-identify with a particular role is that the aspects of your life outside that role don't give you as great a sense of achievement or feeling of being needed. If all you focus on is that particular role, for example, work and your achievements (or lack of), life can soon feel out of balance. Now, when I say balance, I don't mean that everything has to be in equal measure. Maybe a better way to describe it is that life can start to become very small. Having a diverse range of activities in your life can be beneficial on different levels. Different activities require different skills and willingness for engagement. They provide you with different experiences and emotions. They don't all require your attention at the same time, and can offer some stability and constancy when other areas of your life are feeling less stable or more unpredictable.

For example, if all you have to focus on is your work, what happens when work is feeling uncertain? What happens if you become unwell and can't engage in work the way you're used to doing? Believe me, I know what that feels like, and wow, that was a prime opportunity for my self-critic to come to the party and start causing trouble. What if a client decides they no longer want to work with you because what you are providing is not helpful? Or your workplace is restructuring and you're unsure what that means for you? It can be hard to focus your attention elsewhere when it's stressful thinking about work in those situations. Where do you put your attention if you don't have other areas of interest, other areas where you also feel confident and competent or at least know that you're doing okay?

As humans, it is common to want to confirm what we believe to be true. So, if you're feeling inadequate or incompetent at work or in a particular role in your life, then you may look for other things that prove that to be true. If your life is lacking in other areas, then your self-critic might show up and remind you that you don't have an active social life, and you don't even have a hobby. Side note: I've always disliked the question, 'What is your hobby?' Can you legitimately answer, 'Hanging out with people I love and eating great food', or 'Watching reruns of my favourite shows', or 'Reminiscing about when my boy was small enough to fit snugly into my hug.' Your critic will do its best to convince you that you are not enough.

Showing up for yourself can be hard. Particularly if you are someone who has been socialised to be there for others, rather than for yourself. Choosing to prioritise your own needs and wellbeing can bring up a lot of internal discomfort. It's important to recognise the difference between your priorities and someone else's priorities, and to ask yourself, whose priorities are you living by? I get it; you don't want to let people down, disappoint them, have them be mad at you, judge you or not like you. These are really common fears. As humans, we have a fundamental, biologically driven need for belonging. Focusing on yourself signals that you're not focused on others, and this can signal to your brain that there's danger. There's a saying, 'A lone monkey is a dead monkey'. We are designed to be part of the group. Our ancestors' survival depended on it. We have a highly attuned threat system, and based on your own history and experiences, this may be set on extra high alert. Remember the car alarm analogy I gave you earlier?

The reality is that some people will judge you, be mad at you or feel disappointed by you, regardless of what you do, because they are also humans with tricky minds with their own sets of experiences and beliefs. So, how about you don't disappoint yourself, don't get mad at yourself, and don't judge and criticise yourself.

## *Pause*

Take a moment to consider what your biggest struggle is with showing up for yourself?

What shows up when you think about taking care of yourself?

Whose priorities are you living by?

There are no right or wrong answers here, just pay attention to whatever shows up and make some notes if that's helpful. Just remember to be gentle with yourself as you do this.

There's a difference between knowing something and acting on it in a helpful way. You most likely know that taking care of yourself is a good idea. You may have already read books and listened to podcasts that provide you with information on what you could do and why. (Hey, did you know I have a podcast called *Welcome to Self*® and it's all about helping you take care of yourself?) I'm sure you could come up with a whole list of things that would be helpful to do in service of your own wellbeing. So why then do you find it so hard to do those things? I mean they're going to help you, right? Remember that tricky brain we talked about. If behaviour change was easy, we would all just be getting on with it and living our ideal lives. If recognising our own need for care and having the belief that we deserve it was our default, we would all be champions of self-care. Unfortunately, the reality isn't that simple.

If you are focusing on your own needs, you might notice your inner voice telling you, 'Don't be selfish', 'What about the children?' or 'My clients need me to be available'. These are all ways our tricky brain helps us to focus back on the group and not risk our place amongst it. This is just the threat system doing what it is designed to do – keeping you safe. The thing is, we don't live in the times of our ancestors. Being with our group most of the time to avoid danger isn't as necessary as it was back then. It's okay to take time out; in fact, it's important for our nervous systems. We live in a world that we were not designed to live in. We weren't designed for constant stimuli, constant connection via email and smartphones, or the fast pace that our world now moves at. Life has changed so much, and we are more connected and contactable, and multi-tasking far more than previous generations. Now we need to be more intentional about our self-care.

Self-care needs to be an ongoing daily process. Your needs may be different in the morning than in the afternoon, different in different contexts, in different places, with different people and when by yourself. There is no one size fits all with this. Tailor your self-care to suit your individual needs on an ongoing basis. You can develop a plan, though you also need flexibility for when circumstances require different for you and from you. When thinking about showing up for yourself, you can think about it in terms of a *Think, Feel, Do* mentality. You can *Think* about what is happening and what you need in a particular situation. You can check in with how you *Feel* about it, not only the situation but also what shows up for you in relation to the situation. Then you can *Do* what you think would be most helpful given what you know, what you feel and what you're capable of at the time. Notice how I say, 'what you're capable of at the time'? I add this because our tricky brains are very good at switching to self-critic mode and giving us a hard time for things that aren't necessarily within our control. Remember, you can only ever do the best that you can under the circumstances you're in, with the knowledge, skills and resources that you have. It is really easy to fall into a 'should do' pattern without slowing down and considering what impact it has on you if you keep on 'doing' all the time. When you come from a compassionate-self perspective, you can assist yourself to come up with more workable solutions and practices.

I have learnt over the years that the more I slow down my body and breath, the more I can tune out the external and internal noise and access my own wisdom. Gosh, I wish I had learnt it a lot sooner and am grateful that I now have. These are some of the key words I hold in mind for myself: self-reflection, self-awareness, self-compassion, self-care.

**Self-reflection –** Remind yourself to slow down and think about what you need in the current situation. Have you faced this before? Is it a situation that you need to manage by yourself, or can you ask someone for their support, or delegate a particular task? Is this something that needs your attention right now, or can you leave it to a time that suits you better?

**Self-awareness –** Being more aware of your feelings and behaviours in a situation can be helpful in your decision-making. What feelings do you have in relation to this situation? What feelings does it bring up? Have you had similar feelings before? Are these feelings linked to the current situation, or are they triggered by memories of something past? How are you behaving? Is this how you usually behave? Do you want to continue to behave this way? Bring to mind your values and what is meaningful to you. How do your values fit with this situation?

**Self-compassion** – Consider how you would treat a loved one, friend or colleague in this situation. What would be a helpful response? Think about the ways you speak to the people in your life who you love and care about. How do you respond to their suffering? What do you want for them in that moment? What do you do to try to alleviate their suffering? Can you offer yourself this same care, understanding, kindness and compassion?

**Self-care** – Think about the ideal action you'd like to take in this situation. What is a small step towards the outcome you want? Are there any resources you need to help you with this action? How can this be done in a way that honours your own wellbeing?

Initially, it might take you more time to work through situations by asking yourself questions like these, but as you practise, it'll likely save you time and help you avoid making threat-based choices that could steer you away from what really matters to you.

I'd now like to take you through a meditation that will allow you to explore prioritising yourself. This might bring up some discomfort if you're not used to prioritising yourself, so go gently with yourself. You might like to record this on your phone so you can close your eyes and play it back, or use the QR code and I will guide you.

## PRIORITISING YOU

*I invite you to find a comfortable position, ideally with your feet on the floor, in an upright position allowing an open diaphragm. You can open your diaphragm by gently rolling your shoulders up and back. Most important is that you listen to what your body needs and give yourself permission to do that. It might be sitting on a chair or the floor, laying down on the floor or your bed, or in any other position that suits you. Honour your body in a way that feels comfortable. I will be inviting you to imagine different things, and for some people, imagining looks different. It doesn't matter whether you bring to mind complete images, partial images or even just a felt sense of what I am describing. Take a moment to give yourself permission to experience this in whatever way your experience unfolds and know that at any time, you can choose to come out of this practice and return to it as you desire.*

*Take a moment to slow down your breath and gently close your eyes or rest your gaze in front of you. Imagine you are standing in a line with some other people. Look around you. Who is there? Friends, family, clients? Where are you standing in the line? You are all lining up waiting to be served.*

*Now imagine walking past the other people to the front of the line. Notice what thoughts and feelings show up as you walk to the front.*

*You might like to gently place your hand over your heart. If you notice, 'don't push in', 'you shouldn't be at the front', 'other people need this more than you', can you offer yourself the words, 'I matter too', 'It's okay for me to have my needs met', 'It's okay for me to have my needs met first'. Notice what shows up for you as you gently say these words to yourself. Notice the tone of voice you use as you speak to yourself. Notice your breath. If it needs slowing down, then slow it down a little and notice how that feels.*

*Now imagine walking up to the person serving and having your needs met. Then step aside and notice how everyone else is able to move forward and have their needs met too. Notice how you having your needs met hasn't stopped them receiving what they need.*

*What does it feel like to recognise your own needs and realise that your needs don't negatively impact those other people? If your mind starts giving you scenarios where someone else might be negatively impacted by you having your needs met, just notice that and, as best you can, observe those thoughts with curiosity and non-judgement. Spend a few more moments with your breath, just noticing the in-breath and the out-breath.*

*Now start to notice how it feels to be sitting or lying where you are. Notice the points of contact between you and the surface you are on. Notice the sounds around you. Now bring your attention to the feel of the air on your skin. Gently make some small movements with your fingers and*

> *toes. As you feel ready, you can open your eyes, bring your attention back to the place you are in and stretch your body or give your body whatever it needs right now.*

Before moving on, take a moment to reflect on your experience in that meditation. You might want to make some notes about anything that showed up, surprised or shocked you, or any wisdom that appeared during the meditation. Just write whatever you feel inclined to write.

I mentioned earlier that one of my keywords is self-compassion, but what is compassion and how can you cultivate more of it for yourself? Let's look at that next.

*Compassion is not the easy option.
To be willing to move towards suffering
and look it directly in the face
takes courage and strength.*

*You have that courage and strength within you.*

# 8

# *The Courage to Choose Compassion*

I previously had such a toxic relationship with myself, and for most of my life I wasn't even aware of how awful that relationship was. I didn't stop to question the harsh voice in my head or the different types of suffering I was experiencing. I certainly wasn't thinking about how I could prevent the suffering or help myself feel better. Once I learnt about compassion, I started to really embody it and could see the benefits through my own experience, and that of my clients and the health professionals I was training. I knew this was something that would have a huge influence on all aspects of my life. It has created a truly profound shift in my life, and that is why I am so passionate about bringing it into the lives of other people. You could say I've found my passion in compassion.

First, it's important to clarify what compassion is and what it isn't. There are a lot of misconceptions about compassion. People can mistake compassion for something that is weak or soft, something that 'lets you off the hook', or that it's only about being kind. Compassion is strong, wise and courageous. It asks us to be willing to move towards the suffering of ourselves and others, so weak is definitely not a way I would describe it. I believe developing compassion is one of the strongest and most courageous actions we can take.

Before we move on, let's make sure we have a shared understanding of what we're talking about. My preferred definition of compassion is by Professor Paul Gilbert OBE, founder of Compassion Focused Therapy: Compassion is a sensitivity to suffering in self and others with a commitment to alleviate or prevent suffering.

Let's unpack that a little bit. First, you have the sensitivity to suffering – you notice that either you or someone else is suffering. You need to be aware of what is happening, tuned in to the situation and understand what suffering might look like. Then you need to care about the suffering, have empathy for the person, whether that be yourself or someone else. Once you have that awareness and have connected to your caring motivation, you commit to doing something helpful that will ease the suffering and/or put something in place that will prevent further and future suffering.

The other important thing to understand about compassion is that compassion is a motivation, not an emotion or feeling. To help make this clearer, think about these different situations.

1) Watching a child fall off a bicycle and going to help.
    You notice what has happened and recognise the child is distressed. You might experience feelings like shock, concern, maybe some sadness if it's your child and they're upset. You are motivated to help them up, tend to any injuries and comfort them.

2) A firefighter rushing into a burning building to save someone. They are aware of the burning building, recognise the danger and that people are in need of help. They might experience feelings like fear, anxiety, urgency. They are motivated to put out the fire, assist people out of the building and save lives.

See how the feelings are different in these two situations? In both situations there is the motivation to alleviate suffering.

Gilbert describes twelve competencies of compassion. These allow us to either engage with suffering or to take action towards alleviating and preventing suffering. I will briefly take you through these. The six competencies that support engagement with suffering, whether that is ours or someone else's include:

- **Care for wellbeing** – Motivation or willingness to notice suffering and turn towards it rather than look away.
- **Sensitivity** – The ability to look out for suffering and be attentive to that suffering.
- **Sympathy** – The ability to be emotionally connected, attuned and moved by the suffering (ours or that of someone else).
- **Distress tolerance** – The ability to tolerate the emotions that are connected to the suffering.
- **Empathy** – The ability to take the perspective of another, or a different part of yourself. Remember you are multiple versions of self. The ability to imagine 'walking in someone else's shoes' or truly being with and understanding your own experiences and feelings.
- **Non-judgement** – The ability to bring acceptance to a situation and be non-judgemental and non-critical.

The six competencies that support us to respond and take action in a wise and courageous manner include:

- **Attention** – The ability to pay attention to what's helpful. This involves attention training and practising mindfulness.
- **Imagery** – Using imagery and practices like meditation to arouse particular emotions.
- **Reasoning** – Thinking about what will be genuinely helpful.
- **Behaviour** – Behaving in helpful ways. This might sometimes look like doing something you find hard and frightening, helping yourself or others or doing less of something that is not helpful to you or others.
- **Sensory** – Awareness and focusing. Use of breathing practices and our senses to feel grounded and help activate the parasympathetic nervous system.
- **Feeling** – Recognition of complex emotions linked to engagement in suffering and taking action. We often think of kindness when we talk about compassion, but different feelings will be generated depending on the context. For example: Anger about social injustice. Sadness when working with someone at end of life. Anxiety for the firefighter risking their life to save others.

We need to be willing to learn, train and develop these competencies. Good intention won't make the changes; we need to learn to do it differently and take action. We also need to remember that compassion isn't only meant to flow outwards. So many of us are great at the outward flow of compassion, but there are two other important flows of compassion we need to consider. Let's look at all three flows next.

> This is just a brief explanation of these attributes. If you're interested, you can gain a deeper understanding from Professor Paul Gilbert's work. I've added some recommended resources at the end of the book.
>
> The principles and practices of CFT run deep throughout my work. To learn more through individual coaching, the **Welcome to Self®:** *Time to Thrive* group program or to enquire about workshops and speaking opportunities go to https://drhayleydquinn.com

## Three flows of compassion

Self-compassion is something that I believe can truly change the trajectory of your life. However, it's important to know there are three flows of compassion and each of them is important. As women, we tend to be very good at letting compassion flow outward to others, but how easily do you offer compassion to yourself or let yourself receive compassion from others? Do you even recognise it when it's offered to you?

'If your compassion does not include yourself, it is incomplete.' I love this quote by Jack Kornfield, and I couldn't agree more.

Let's explore these three flows in a bit more detail and reflect on how they show up in your life. Remember to check in with yourself and engage to the level that feels right for you in the moment. You might want to make some notes if that feels helpful.

### Compassion to others – I see your suffering and I want to assist

Like I said, offering compassion to others doesn't seem to be difficult for most women. We are taught from a young age to tend to the needs of others and to notice others' suffering, often before our own. However, this can be problematic if it's the only flow of compassion. Are you someone who finds themselves constantly giving out to others? When you do this and don't take the time to care for yourself, it can leave you depleted, and when you feel depleted, you can start to form resentments and maybe even become hostile to others. This can then play into how you feel about yourself and what you feel you deserve. It can be quite a cycle you can find yourself in.

## *Pause*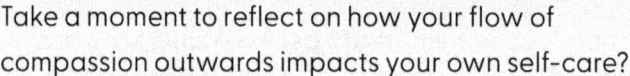

Take a moment to reflect on how your flow of compassion outwards impacts your own self-care?

- Do you find it easy to offer compassion to others?
- Do you see yourself as a highly compassionate person?
- Do you ever feel resentful about how much time you spend thinking about and helping others?
- Are you so busy offering compassion to others that it prevents you from taking care of yourself?

What stood out to you about your outward flow of compassion? Let's now look at self-compassion.

### Self-compassion – I see my suffering and I want to behave in ways to alleviate my suffering

Many women have not been taught to recognise their own needs, let alone tend to them. In a world where the messaging is, 'You're here to take care of others', 'Your needs don't matter so much', 'Your problems aren't worthy of financial funding' and 'Your rights aren't as important as those of men', it's hardly surprising you struggle to prioritise yourself and take the time and space you need to focus on your wellbeing and happiness.

## *Pause*

Take a moment to reflect on your own experience of self-compassion. Allow yourself some time to think about how you relate to yourself.

- Is your tone towards yourself kind, calm and encouraging, or does it tend to be more hostile, critical and cold?
- Do you get caught up in calling yourself names?
- Would you consider yourself more of a friend or a bully to yourself?
- How do you recognise what you need?
- How and what do you offer to yourself when these needs show up?
- Do you think the way you treat yourself is helpful or harmful?

What stood out to you about your level of self-compassion? Let's look at the third flow, compassion from others, next.

## FROM SELF-NEGLECT TO SELF-COMPASSION

***Compassion from others*** – You see my suffering, and you want to help me

Compassion from others can come in many different forms. It could be as simple as someone noticing you're busy and offering to make you a cup of tea, so you can stay hydrated, or someone offering to attend a medical appointment with you so you don't feel so alone. It might involve someone advocating for you when you can't do that for yourself. It might look like someone taking care of your daily tasks while you recover from illness. There are so many ways it can show up in your life, and I've worked with many people who struggle to receive this flow of compassion. This was the flow of compassion that took me by surprise after I had developed a strong compassionate self and mistakenly thought I had nailed the whole compassion thing. Let me tell you about the time I was presenting a talk in New York and the huge compassion lesson I was fortunate enough to learn.

> *I had been invited to present at the* Compassionate Mind Summit and Retreat *and the evening before the event, all the speakers attended a dinner at the hosts' home. As we headed outside, I managed to misstep the stairs, twist my ankle and fall. I was surrounded by people who were there to present about compassion, so as I'm sure you can imagine, they were kind and compassionate people and rushed to my aid.*
>
> *My internal response shocked me. As they offered help, my mind was silently swearing and screaming for them all to get away from me. I was thrown straight into my threat system. I was telling them, 'I'm okay', even though I wasn't. I was in excruciating pain and couldn't even stand up by myself. I had to accept that I needed help and would continue to need help across the next*

few days. The discomfort, embarrassment and shame that coursed through me at times felt almost unbearable, but I knew I had no choice but to surrender to the generous help of these compassionate others.

The venue where we were presenting was up a flight of steep stairs and I had to succumb to being assisted up the stairs and to people fetching food for me, not just once but every mealtime, and them helping me in the various ways I needed. When my time to present arrived, I sat in front of the audience with my foot resting on a chair ready to speak. I felt so vulnerable, and also grateful, to the people there and for the experience I was having. Now that might sound a bit strange, given the pain I was in, but that experience allowed me to see that whilst I had developed a beautiful compassionate relationship with myself and had no problem offering compassion to others, receiving compassion from others was something I obviously struggled with. It was a very humbling experience and one that allowed me to practise receiving compassion from others. This practice would continue to serve me well. It really highlighted the importance of all three flows of compassion.

## *Pause*

Take a moment to reflect on your own experience of receiving compassion.

- Are you able to accept compassionate assistance when you need or want it?
- Do you reject it, perhaps due to feeling like you don't deserve it?

- *Do you recognise when you are being offered compassion from someone else?*
- *Do you have someone you consider to be a compassionate other in your life?*
- *Are you able to ask for support and compassion from someone else?*

What stood out to you about receiving compassion from others? If you are constantly giving out to others and struggle to welcome in, or even recognise, the flow of compassion from others, you can find yourself feeling like people don't care so much without recognising your own blocks to this flow of compassion.

**THREE FLOWS OF COMPASSION**

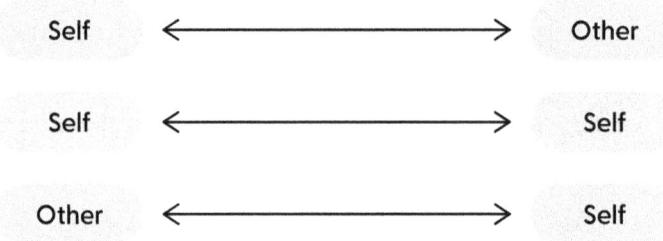

Remember to think about all three flows of compassion. It's hard to truly take care of yourself if compassion is only flowing outwards. Most, if not all, the women I know are extremely good at offering compassion to other people. However, when it comes to self-compassion that can be a different story. It can be a real struggle. Don't forget the importance of receiving compassion from others either. This again can be a huge struggle for people, but with practice, this can change.

Hopefully, reading this book will increase your desire to take care of yourself, and you'll finish this knowing that you are a worthwhile and valuable human who deserves care, compassion from yourself and others, and a bloody great life!

*So why is the relationship I have with myself so important?*

*I'm glad you asked.*

How you see and treat yourself can have a ripple effect on so many other things you do. It can impact the choices you make, what you think you deserve, who you allow into your life and what you will tolerate. If you don't think you deserve to go after your dreams and goals, then why would you even try? If you don't believe you deserve to be treated with respect and dignity from others, why would you bother putting boundaries in place or let people know that how they're treating you is unacceptable?

If you don't know what personal boundaries are, first, please don't judge yourself for that. If you've never been taught about boundaries, how are you expected to know? I have worked with so many people over the years who, at the start of our work together, had no understanding of boundaries. If you want to learn more about how to set boundaries and talk about them with other people, we'll be looking at that a little bit later. You can choose to jump ahead now or keep reading and know that the information is waiting for you when you get there. I encourage you to keep reading though, because we're going to continue with some practices to help you develop a more compassionate mind, and that will help you with any boundary setting later.

*Compassion flows out to others.*
*Compassion flows in from those around me.*
*Compassion flows within me.*

## Cultivating a compassionate mind

It takes ongoing practice to cultivate a mind that defaults to compassion. The more you practise, the easier it becomes to access this way of thinking and being with yourself. We are going to do another practice now. You might like to record yourself reading this so you can then close your eyes and play it back, or you can use the QR code and I will guide you.

> **CULTIVATING A COMPASSIONATE MIND**
>
> *I invite you to find a comfortable position, ideally with your feet on the floor, in an upright position allowing an open diaphragm. You can open your diaphragm by gently rolling your shoulders up and back. Most important is that you listen to what your body needs and give yourself permission to do that. It might be sitting on a chair or the floor, laying down on the floor or your bed, or in any other position that suits you. Honour your body in a way that feels comfortable.*
>
> *I will be inviting you to imagine different things, and for some people, imagining looks different. It doesn't matter whether you bring to mind complete images, partial images or even just a felt sense of what I am describing. Take a*

moment to give yourself permission to experience this in whatever way your experience unfolds, and know that at any time you can choose to come out of this practice and return to it as you desire.

If it feels comfortable, go ahead and close your eyes or gently rest your gaze in front of you. Notice how it feels to be sitting or laying where you are. Notice any points of contact between you and the surface you are on. Just take a moment to make any micro-movements your body might need. Let your mind just momentarily drift to the sounds around you.

I now invite you to gently bring your attention to your breath, just noticing your in-breath and your out-breath. Notice the rhythm and the pace of your breath and start to slow your breath down a bit, maintaining equal in- and out-breaths. Now, slow your breath a little more and as you do this, just notice any changes in your body and your mind. On your next out-breath, you can quietly say to yourself, 'mind slowing down.' And on your next out-breath, 'body slowing down.' All the time, just knowing that when you're breathing in, you're breathing in, and when you're breathing out, you're breathing out.

Your mind may wander as you do this and that's perfectly normal. If you notice this happening, you can choose to gently bring your attention back to your breath. Just take a moment to experience whatever it is you're experiencing right now. No need to change it. Just be curious about what it's like to be you right now in this moment. Bring gentle curiosity to any thoughts, feelings or physical sensations.

Now bring to mind your day ahead and as you do this, notice your breath. Notice if it's slow or perhaps it might *quicken. If it quickens, just take a moment to slow your breath down again.*

*Think about what you have ahead of you today. The things that are important. The things that perhaps feel important but maybe are not so important. Is that sense of importance motivated by having to meet other people's needs or keeping everyone else happy?*

*Maybe you have certain tasks that you haven't finished because they don't feel quite good enough yet. But maybe they actually are good enough. Can you allow them to be good enough and let go of the need for them to be perfect?*

*Bring to mind the things that perhaps you could set aside to make room for yourself today.*

*Now take a moment to think about what you need today. Not anyone else, just you and what you need.*

*If you could be your most compassionate self, with wisdom, strength and courage and a deep sense of caring, what would you offer yourself today? Imagine what it would be like to accept that offer and have what you need.*

*Spend a few more moments resting in the soothing rhythm of your breath. Allow these moments to be for you. As you breathe in, imagine you are strengthening your self-compassion. As you breathe out, imagine you are releasing any feelings of not deserving compassion.*

*Start to notice how it feels to be sitting or lying where you are. Notice the points of contact between you and the surface you are on. Allow your mind to go to the sounds around you. Start to make some micro movements, perhaps moving your fingers and toes. As you feel ready, you can open your eyes, bringing your attention back to the place*

> *you are in, and stretch your body or give your body whatever it needs right now.*

This is a practice you can use on a regular basis to help cultivate your compassionate mind. There are numerous practices that can help you do this. The main thing is to do some sort of practice. This can range from a brief check-in with yourself using a friendly voice through to formal meditation practices.

Another practical and helpful way to continue to cultivate your compassionate mind, and to change the relationship you have with yourself, is to engage in perspective taking and compassionate reframing. We're going to look at that next. If you need to take a break, make yourself a drink, have a bathroom stop, or have a few moments to yourself before moving on, allow yourself to do that. Little check-ins with yourself like this and taking action on what you need also help you develop a compassionate relationship with yourself.

## Compassionate reframing: a new way to speak to yourself

Compassionate reframing is about looking at a situation from a different perspective using the lens of compassion to adjust how we see a situation, and ultimately how we take care of and speak to ourselves during those times. When talking to ourselves, our default can be a self-critical (threat-based) response. If we can reframe these responses to ones that are more compassionate, we are more likely to make decisions and engage in behaviours that are helpful to our present and future selves.

Wouldn't it be nicer if you spoke to yourself the way you speak to people you love and care about? Please make sure your name is on the list of people you care about.

I have included some examples below, highlighting a threat-based response, a compassionate alternative and the reality of why this can be so difficult. You can then reflect on the example in relation to your own experience, and I'll also invite you to practise writing some for yourself.

### Example One

**Threat Based:** *I'm a caring person; I 'should' be able to be compassionate to myself.*

**Compassion Based:** Being self-compassionate can be really hard. There are things about my own history and experiences that make this difficult for me. I can keep practising and it will get easier.

**Reasoning:** Just because you are a caring person doesn't mean you don't find things challenging. You may have survived trauma. You may struggle with anxiety and depression. You may have a very harsh self-critic. You might just be having a very hard day. As a human being, you're not immune to these things. Practising self-compassion can be tricky. I say 'practice' because that's exactly what it is – a practice. Sometimes it might feel easier than other times; sometimes it might feel damn near impossible. As best you can, try to remind yourself that you are a human first and like all humans, you have a tricky mind and sometimes things are hard. Try not to 'should' all over yourself. See if you can find a more gentle and helpful way to support yourself, or reach out to others for support.

## Pause

What is my biggest challenge with being self-compassionate?

**Example Two**

**Threat Based:** *I can't admit I am struggling; other people rely on me, and I 'should' know how to manage this myself.*

**Compassion Based:** I am human. Life's struggles and/or mental illness do not discriminate. It is okay and important for me to reach out for support from others.

**Reasoning:** 'I should know how to manage this myself' is probably one of the most unhelpful phrases in our vocabulary. We are social beings; we are meant to be connected to others and community. Supporting one another is such an important part of our care and wellbeing. I'll keep saying this – being in a role that supports others, whether this is in your personal or professional life, does not immunise you from life's struggles, mental illness, tragedies or generally feeling crappy. You deserve support just like everyone else. It is so important that you can access safe, supportive and understanding people and services. I recognise that adequate and accessible services are not always available. This is a systemic problem, not because you don't deserve help. You don't need to know how to manage everything by yourself. Please do your best to reach out, stay connected and let someone know you're struggling.

## *Pause*

Where did I learn that I have to do it all by myself?

What is it about my history that would help me make sense of this?

**Example Three**

**Threat Based:** *I can only take a day off if I'm really sick or I'll be putting more burden on others.*

**Compassion Based:** It is important for me to take care of my mental and physical health. I am deserving of the care and concern I give to others. I can notice my thoughts about burdening others and still take care of myself.

**Reasoning:** First, define 'sick enough'. Second, you're sick; it's okay to take time off. When we take time off to care for ourselves, not only are we recognising, acknowledging and meeting our own needs, we are also modelling good self-care for our family, our clients and others. I'm not just talking about physical health here. Let's reduce the stigma of mental health too. If you are struggling with physical or mental health, you need to take time out to care for yourself. And if you're struggling cognitively and/or emotionally, you're not going to be effective in your work and will find things far easier to manage once you've rested and recovered. Please honour yourself as best you can when you're sick and give yourself the time and space you need.

> ## *Pause*
>
> What do I notice when I think about taking time off to look after my wellbeing? How sick do I have to be before I allow myself space and time to rest and recuperate?

**Example Four:**

**Threat Based:** *I have to be available all the time or I am letting other people down.*

**Compassion Based:** I can choose when I'm available to others and allow myself to be available for myself and the things I'd like to do. I can choose not to let myself down.

**Reasoning:** You can't possibly be available all the time, nor do you need to be. Setting clear boundaries with others is helpful for everyone. Having time out for yourself to focus on the important aspects of your life is needed. Give yourself permission to include yourself on your priority list. Remind yourself that your needs matter too.

> ## *Pause*
>
> What do I notice when I think about not always being available for other people?

## Example Five

**Threat Based:** *I'm a parent/carer/helping professional; it's my job to always be caring.*

**Compassion Based:** I recognise the importance of including myself in my desire to care. I am a human first. Being a parent/carer/helping professional does not define all of who I am.

**Reasoning:** You've likely heard the saying, 'Put on your own oxygen mask first before helping others.' If you take some small moments to focus in on what you need and then allow yourself to meet those needs, it's likely you'll be in a better position to help others. You're more likely to be helpful if you are feeling refreshed, energised, healthy and happy, rather than exhausted, depleted and possibly resentful.

What I'm saying here is please don't forget yourself in the mix. You matter too.

### *Pause*

What in my history would help me understand why I might find it hard to prioritise my needs over someone else's?

Now it's your turn. Using the headings below, think of some of the threat-based things you say to yourself and then come up with a compassionate alternative. If you want to reflect on the reasoning, go ahead and do that too.

### Practice One

Threat Based: _____
Compassion Based: _____
Reasoning: _____

### Practice Two

Threat Based: _____
Compassion Based: _____
Reasoning: _____

### Practice Three

Threat Based: _____
Compassion Based: _____
Reasoning: _____

### Practice Four

Threat Based: _____
Compassion Based: _____
Reasoning: _____

### Practice Five

Threat Based: _____
Compassion Based: _____
Reasoning: _____

Now you've done that, reflect on how easy or challenging you found it, and how it felt coming up with the compassionate statements. As you're practising this new way of relating to yourself, please make sure you go gently with yourself. People who know me, recognise that this is something I say a lot. I believe going gently with yourself is a helpful way to live your life. When I use the term gently, I don't mean you can't be assertive or stand strong; not at all. You can be mindful of how you take care of yourself during the times you need to be assertive; you can be gentle with yourself no matter what you're doing. You can treat yourself with care, kindness and compassion in all things you do.

It's not about being passive, quiet or a soft touch. It's about recognising your worth, caring about yourself and supporting yourself in all that you do. It's also not about always getting it right. Sometimes you'll forget to do things a particular way, you'll struggle to live in line with your values, and you'll have times when you're harsh to yourself. When you notice this, you can still be gentle with yourself and remind yourself you're human.

*Space for yourself doesn't just show up and magically happen; you have to create it on purpose.*

# 9

## *Time to Prioritise You*

Sometimes in life, you experience something that prompts you to make changes. This might be one big event; you know, the type that gives you no choice but to see what is right in front of you. That was me when I hit full burnout. There had been many signs for many years that I didn't pay attention to. Then burnout knocked the air out of me, forced me to slow down and listen, and gave me no choice but to pay attention and make some changes.

For you, this might have already happened too, or you might be noticing small events, thoughts or feelings and you're not really listening to them yet. These experiences might come in the form of more regular tears, an emotional breakthrough triggered by something you read, a conversation you have or something you witness. This then creates an opening and an invitation for you to walk through, allowing you to find yourself in a new place within; a place from which you can more deeply know yourself and start to do things differently.

## Pause

Think back to a time you might have had one of these experiences. Think about what you were doing and how you felt. Ask yourself:

- *Did I accept the invitation and allow myself to occupy a new version of myself?*
- *If so, how did that feel? If not, what do I think has stopped me from taking that step?*

I know choosing yourself can be hard. It can feel selfish, you can feel undeserving, or you can struggle to even know how to do that. I'm here to tell you it's not selfish and you are absolutely deserving. These next sections will give you some ideas about how you can start choosing you.

Quick tip before we move on – when we want to do something differently, it's good to take it step by step. Start small and don't try to change everything all at once. That just becomes overwhelming, activates your threat system (red circle) and makes it all harder. You don't need things to be harder; some change is hard enough already, so go gently with yourself.

Here are three small practices that you can try to help you choose you:

1) When making a drink for you and someone else, practise pouring yours first – radical, I know! The number of women who have looked at me shocked when I suggest this, and then realise they have **never** poured their own drink first. This saddens me so much.

2) When making a shopping list – if you do that – or when someone else in the household is making one, see if you can add the things you want to the list first.

3) Add your breaks and holidays to your calendar before opening it up to other people. Now, I appreciate that if you have children or other care responsibilities, there might be some non-negotiable dates for your calendar, but once you've added those, make sure you add yours next.

## When you have a lot to do, slow it down!

I attended many workshops delivered by Dr Kelly Wilson – co-founder of *Acceptance and Commitment Therapy*, and at the start of many of Kelly's workshops, I'd hear him say, 'We have a lot to get through today, so we need to go slowly.' People always laugh, yet he really means what he's saying; not as a joke, but as a reminder to us that the slower we go, the quicker we tend to get to the place we need to be. Whether that is to answer a question, to get to the end of a project, or to understand the core of our experiences. We live in a fast-paced world that encourages and rewards rushing, racing and competitiveness, yet we are not designed to live in a world like that. These messages are everywhere, social media, billboards, in our everyday conversations at work and perhaps within our homes. So, it's not surprising that if we're starting to feel burnt out or if we're feeling unsure of our capabilities, we try to do more, be more, achieve more to help us feel better about ourselves. What I do know, though, is we can't work ourselves harder to avoid or recover from burnout. We need to take care of ourselves and our nervous system.

Our nervous system is very complex. I'm going to give you a very simplified explanation that will be enough for right now. We have a sympathetic and a parasympathetic nervous system. I like to think of the sympathetic nervous system as the accelerator on a car. It prepares our body for action, readying us for our fight/flight response. On the other hand, I like to think of the parasympathetic nervous system as the brakes on a car. This part of our nervous system calms our body down and allows us to settle into rest and digest and soothing.

We have a nerve in our body called the vagus nerve. It's the longest cranial nerve and is sometimes called the wandering nerve due to the extensive span throughout the body. It travels from the brainstem through the neck, chest and abdomen, supplying nerves to multiple organs along the way. The vagus nerve influences functions like heart rate, digestion, breathing and mood. It is a key part of our parasympathetic nervous system. When the vagus nerve is stimulated, it increases vagal tone, and this helps us more effectively activate our soothing system, which as we talked about earlier, makes it easier for us to access our wisdom and make helpful decisions about what we want.

Let's take a moment now to slow down with a few soothing breaths, inhaling and exhaling for a count of four, to help stimulate your vagus nerve and activate your soothing system (green circle). Don't be tempted to skip this. You can keep reading very soon.

*Inhale ... two, three, four*
*Exhale ... two, three, four*
*Inhale ... two, three, four*
*Exhale ... two, three, four*
*Inhale ... two, three, four*
*Exhale ... two, three, four*

*Inhale ... two, three, four*
*Exhale ... two, three, four*
*Inhale ... two, three, four*
*Exhale ... two, three, four*

See how just five soothing breaths allow you to feel different. As well as deep breathing, there are other ways to help increase vagal tone including humming, singing and gargling, exercise, progressive muscle relaxation, tapping the midpoint of your chest and gently massaging behind your ear or gently tugging your earlobe.

Okay, now let's think about your roles and how you organise your life. Reflecting on why you chose a particular role in life or career path can help clarify your motivation. It can also help you stay committed when things feel challenging. Understanding what you do and don't enjoy, or what is currently helpful or harmful about the way you engage in your work and life, can allow you to think about what needs to change and what you might like to do more of. Having a career/business that fits you and your individual life circumstances can make all the difference to the longevity, sustainability and enjoyment of your work. Remember that your life circumstances can change over time, and these reflections are not just something you do once and then set and forget. It is important to recognise what you need at different stages of your life and career. At some point in your life, you might need or want to work full time, and this may change to a need or desire for part-time work, more diversity in your work or to cease work when your circumstances change.

Your needs in the early stages of your career or a new role will differ to those when you are more advanced in your career or role. Your needs as a working parent will differ from before you had children, or when you are parenting older children. If you're managing health concerns, you will need different things at different times. If you are in a personal caring role for someone, your needs will be different compared to not being in that caring role. Creating a life that works for you involves reflecting on what you need and want and finding the right way for you, rather than trying to fit yourself into some 'imagined right way'.

Start exploring ways that work for you. There is no one right way to do something in life. Different things work for different situations and different people. We can get so caught up in looking for the elusive 'right way' rather than looking for the way that suits us at any particular time. Even when we find a way that suits our needs and wants, it doesn't mean that it will always be how we need or want it to be. We need to be flexible in our approach and recognise that things might change over time, between situations and depending on how we are feeling. There is no one right way to work with clients, run your business, organise your household, take care of yourself or be in relationships with other people. Allow yourself the freedom to explore what works for you at different times, with different people and in different circumstances.

*The thing I love most about choice is that you can always make another one.*

This is one of my favourite things to say to myself and my clients. It helps remind me that nothing is set in stone. If I make a choice about something, I'm doing that based on my current circumstances with the information I have at the time. If what I choose doesn't work well or things change, I can make another choice. Don't hold yourself to a rigid way of being. Be willing to change things when they are no longer working for you. Someone else's right way isn't the way it needs to be, no matter how appealing it might look from the outside, or how credible they might sound. Get to know yourself and learn what works best for you, then see if you can give yourself permission to choose your way. *Psychological flexibility* is your ability to be present to what is happening in your life, to have a willingness to be with any uncomfortable feelings or thoughts, and to take action that aligns with your values, even when it feels challenging. If you can develop psychological flexibility, you're more able to make the changes that will benefit you and allow you to create the life you want.

## *Pause*

I invite you to think about how you want your life to be. You might find it helpful to refer back to the values exercise you did earlier. Spend some time writing down your answers if that feels helpful.

- *Reflect on the main roles you hold and what you enjoy or value about them.*
- *Think about the areas in your life that feel depleting, or you don't enjoy.*
- *What is important to you, both in your work and your personal life?*
- *How important is it to you that you take care of yourself so you can do these things?*

As you look back on these reflections, what do you notice? Is there anything that stands out? Notice any thoughts or feelings that show up as you read over your answers and remember to connect with your compassionate self. Connecting with your compassionate self will help you to be more understanding and respond to yourself in a helpful manner.

Often when I work with people to help them prioritise themselves more, we come up against a common theme. A lot of their time is spent focusing on other people's needs and not wanting to let people down, so they say yes more often than they'd like to and subsequently miss out on doing things they wanted or needed to do for themselves. Learning to say no and being willing to be with any discomfort that comes along with that can be helpful in reprioritising how you want to live.

Let's look at what might show up for you when it comes to saying no and how you can start to say no to others and not just yourself.

## Saying no to others so you can say yes to yourself

'No' is one of the smallest words in the English language, and yet it can be one of the hardest for people to say. I often have conversations with people about the fact that it's not that they're not great at saying no; they're just saying no to the wrong person. Often when I speak to others – clients, friends and family – they've spent years saying no to themselves from a motivation of fear. Fear of judgement from others, fear of rejection from others or a desire to please the people around them in order to be liked. Does this sound familiar?

It's understandable; you're a social being and have a biological need to belong. The fear of rejection can feel dangerous and quickly activate your threat system (red circle). Remember that saying: 'a lone monkey is a dead monkey'? For our ancestors, being separated from the group was extremely dangerous. They relied on being together for their survival. This fear is built into your DNA. So go easy on yourself if you find yourself getting caught up in people-pleasing. Recognising it is a great first step towards changing it.

Some of the times when you're saying yes to somebody else, you have to say no to yourself about something. I'm not saying that happens all the time; sometimes a yes to somebody else would also be a yes to yourself. For example, if somebody asked you to present a training session and they are paying you for your time, or you're invited to attend a meeting that could be mutually beneficial at a time when you don't have any other plans, then saying yes to them is also saying yes to yourself. However, you can find yourself in situations that are quite different. For example, if somebody asks if you could see them at 5.00 pm and you normally finish work at 5.00 pm, you will benefit from thinking about what else you might have planned for that time. You may have plans to attend a personal appointment, or to go to an event, or you may have planned a date with your partner or a friend. On these occasions, saying yes to that person would mean saying no to yourself and the plans that are important to you. Still, many people choose to say yes to the person asking over the plans they have made for themselves. They change their own plans and inconvenience themselves so they can meet the needs of the other. This can lead to resentment, impact the relationships in your life and reinforce your belief that you are there for the service of others and your needs are secondary.

Here's a quick tip I share with friends and clients. If there are times in your day that you know you'll regret saying yes to someone else if you add in an appointment or other commitment, try adding the word RESENTMENT to your calendar at those times. That way, when someone asks if you're free and you go to check, you'll have a handy little reminder about how you'll feel if you say yes.

## *Pause*

Take a moment to think about how often you say 'Yes' to others and 'No' to yourself?

Now we're going to tune into how it feels to say 'No' to someone else.

I invite you to close your eyes for a moment and imagine yourself saying 'No' to someone. Pick anyone you want, maybe a friend, colleague, client or family member (or do this exercise a few times with different people in mind). Notice how it feels in your body when you say 'No' to them. Also notice any thoughts and stories that show up. Take a moment to write these down. You might also want to think about or draw your three circles for each situation. It's all practice.

## *Pause*

I now invite you to set aside some time and ask yourself the following questions. You can also make a note of anything else that shows up for you as you do this.

- *What or who do I need to say no to so I can allow myself the time and space I need or want?*
- *Are there certain tasks that I need to set aside and say no to?*

- *Are there any particular people I need to say no to?*
- *Am I willing to be with any discomfort that shows up when I say no to others? If not, why not?*
- *How much longer am I willing to put up with the discomfort when I say no to myself? The missing out on things, the overwhelm, the resentment.*

Write down the things you would like to say no to, even if you have already said yes to them. This is about being clear and honest with yourself about what you do and don't want to do.

Now write down all the things you have been sacrificing for yourself due to saying yes to other people and things. I've also given you some additional questions to ask yourself.

- Who do I tend to always say yes to? Why do I think that is?
- What would be different if I said no? What is my biggest fear about this?
- What is one small thing that I can do for myself that would allow me to start saying yes to myself more often?

If you can learn to recognise when you want to say no to someone else so you can say yes to yourself, you can start to live more authentically and build a life that suits you and how you want to live. I have got to a place in my life where for the overwhelming majority of the time, I no longer say yes to something out of obligation, fear of not being liked or disappointing someone. The reality is that sometimes in life we are going to disappoint people, and some people might not like us no matter what we do. I figure I might as well live my one precious life in a way that feels right for me. When I say yes to someone, I know I won't feel resentful, and they can trust that if I've said yes, I didn't really mean no but was too scared or polite to say no to them. I accept that I am responsible for myself, my choices and my satisfaction with my life. For me to create a life that allows me to thrive, I need to make choices based on my values and priorities, rather than trying to squeeze myself into someone else's version of how my life should be. It's the same for you; the choices you make, the way you treat yourself and the people you spend time with and how they treat you, all impact your overall wellbeing and how your life feels.

## Who are you spending time with, and most importantly, do you want to?

It is worth thinking about who you spend your time with. Remember, this is a choice you make, even if sometimes it doesn't feel that way. You don't have to spend time with everyone who asks you. Not everyone is entitled to your time. Be choosy. Your time is precious. It's also not realistic to think that you will be the right fit for everyone either. I remind myself that not everyone will like me, and I have to be okay with that. I mean, I don't like everyone I meet. There may be some people in your life now who you feel obligated to spend time with, and making changes to that could feel too big right now. That's okay. Let's start small. I find taking small steps far less overwhelming, and it keeps you out of your threat system, allowing you to move forward more easily.

The people you surround yourself with can have a huge impact on how you feel, both emotionally and physically, and on the choices you make. If you're surrounded by supportive people who encourage you when you need encouragement and are comfortable enough in themselves to celebrate you when you have achieved something, no matter how big or small, you're far more likely to try new things, pursue your dreams and create a life you love. On the other hand, if you're surrounded by critics or even people who show no interest in or care about what you're doing, it can dampen your spirits and lead you to shrinking your dreams, not sharing your wins and feeling less capable of achieving what you want.

This is an opportunity for you to think about the different people in your life and what you do and don't enjoy about this. You might notice some negative or unexpected feelings showing up when you do this. Please go gently with yourself. Be really honest with yourself here. Having negative thoughts and feelings about someone does not, I repeat, does not make you a bad person. There's a reason for how you're thinking and feeling, even if it's just that they're not your vibe and you don't really know why. Be mindful that these are times that your self-critic can show up, so do your best to bring compassion to your experience.

## *Pause*

I invite you to spend some time reflecting on the following prompts and making some notes for yourself. Remember to check in with yourself and engage to the level that feels right for you in this moment.

- *Who are the people I enjoy spending time with and why?*
- *What do I usually do with the people I enjoy spending time with?*

- *Who are the people I don't enjoy spending time with and why?*
- *What do I usually do with the people I don't enjoy spending time with?*
- *What changes would I like to make to who I am spending time with?*

For example: Are there certain people you'd like to spend more time with, less or no time with, or do different things with?

Once you have a greater understanding of yourself, what you do and don't enjoy and who you enjoy spending your time with, you can start to make changes. This will likely require setting some boundaries. One of the ways you can take better care of yourself is through healthy, flexible and helpful boundary setting, so let's have a chat about boundaries next. If now feels like a good time for you to take a break, honour what you need. You can always pick this back up again soon.

*Surround yourself with people who treat you kindly, inspire you, encourage you, and celebrate your successes, no matter how small, and those who stay close and support you when you fall and life feels tough.*

## Boundaries

Boundaries are invisible guidelines and parameters you can set for yourself. They show people what is and what isn't acceptable when it comes to being in a relationship with one another. Boundaries are relevant whether this is an intimate, personal or professional relationship. Boundaries also serve as a trust builder when you apply them to yourself.

Remember, boundaries are containing for everyone. They assist us all to feel safe. The problem is that it is often easier said than done, particularly if you haven't spent time reflecting on why these things are hard for you. Think about your own history and how your own experiences can help you make sense of why this is challenging for you.

It can be easy to dismiss or ignore your own feelings when focusing on others. It is important to include yourself in your caregiving. When you're telling yourself time and time again that you need to be there to take care of others, can you tell yourself that when you take care of yourself you can return later to take care of them? If you're continually neglecting your own needs, wants and desires and not taking care of yourself, this can lead to burnout and an inability to take care of anyone, yourself included. If you recognise yourself as a people-pleaser, be aware of your own feelings when someone is asking you to do something you don't want to do. Being aware of your own stories and beliefs, and noticing when these show up, allows you to remain firm with your boundaries. This takes practice, so go gently with yourself whilst you are learning to do this. Just do your best to set and express your boundaries in any given situation. At the end of the day, your best is the most you can do.

As a caring individual, particularly when you've been socialised to care for others, you can get caught up in worrying about other people's problems. So, how can you manage this when something isn't your responsibility, yet you feel so drawn to help?

- Know your limits
- Check your expectations of both other people and yourself
- Remind yourself where the responsibility belongs
- Think about what you can and can't do, and focus on what you can do
- Acknowledge that it is difficult when you are motivated to help
- Be with your discomfort, validate how you feel and support yourself with compassionate self-talk
- Physical soothing (for example, hand on heart, soothing rhythm breathing)
- Focus on other things that are fun and/or meaningful

So, how can you take care of yourself when the discomfort of setting boundaries shows up, and help yourself take compassionate action rather than succumb to fear-based decision making? I've always found it helpful to have 'scripts' for life and 'policies' for work to refer back to. For example, in business or work, being able to say to someone, 'I will have to decline this as our policy is XYZ', can feel easier than saying, 'I'm not doing that for you.' When developing these scripts for your life and/or policies and practices for your work, it is important to develop these from your wise, calm, compassionate self. Connect with your values and remember yourself as a whole human being, not just the role that you're in for the particular situation. This way, you have something to lean into when you are struggling to enforce or maintain your boundaries.

Boundaried responses don't have to be long and drawn out. They can be succinct and offered in a way that is kind, clear and compassionate. Here are a few examples you can use to get you started. Feel free to adapt these so they fit with how you speak.

*Someone invites you to an event and you don't want to go.*
'I appreciate the invitation, but no thank you.'
Remember, you don't have to explain your reasoning to others.

*A client wants you to work outside your normal hours.*
'I don't work during those times, but I'm happy to find an appointment for you during my available work hours.'

*Someone asks you to look after their child (or pet), but you don't want to or the time clashes with something else.*
'I'd love to help (only say that if you really would), but I am already committed/busy at that time.'

*You're feeling unwell and your child/family member asks you for something.*
'I'm not feeling well, so you'll need to get that yourself.'
If the person isn't capable of helping themselves, say, 'I'm not feeling well so you'll need to ask [insert name] to help you.'

## *Pause*

Take a moment to think about who or where you have the most difficulty setting boundaries.

- *What shows up for me when I think about setting boundaries, or do I not even think about it in those situations or with those people?*
- *What do I think would be different if I were able to set boundaries in those situations or with those people?*
- *What internal resources (e.g. increased confidence, regulated nervous system) do I need to help me set the boundaries?*
- *What external resources (e.g. support from someone else, electronic communication) do I need to help me set the boundaries?*

Living in a busy world means we end up with competing demands. We can get caught in the language of 'need' and 'want'. When the 'need' gets priority, our boundaries can be compromised. This can be tricky because sometimes what looks and sounds like a need is actually a want. Imagine a situation where someone says, 'I *need* to see you' and you've been thinking, 'I *want* to have some time having fun with my friend.' It's likely your mind is going to prioritise the *need* of the other person over the *want* of your own. The thing is, the request from the other person is also a want. They want to see you. Unless it's an emergency, they don't actually need to see you. They could see you when you're next available.

By being aware of this use of language, we are more able to tune in and check whether what is being asked is a need or a want. When we slow down, activate our soothing system (green circle) and take into account our own needs and wants, we can make decisions from a soothed, calm and wise mind as opposed to making decisions out of fear and people-pleasing, and ultimately neglecting our needs.

In the following table are some scenarios. I want you to think about whether they are needs or wants. As you go through these, remember some may be both needs and wants.

| Situation | Need or Want or Both |
|---|---|
| I need a coffee. | |
| I need an appointment with you because I'm catching up with a friend and can't come on Monday. | |
| I need to take a break from work. | |
| I need to do a training in [insert training]. | |
| I need to pick up my child at 3.00 pm. | |
| I need to buy groceries so we can cook. | |
| I need to buy chocolate. | |

Can you see how recognising the language used can be helpful in determining whether something is really a priority, or just someone dressing up a want as a need so it seems more important? When you're more aware of what is being asked of you, how you feel about it and what you want to do, it makes expressing your boundaries that bit easier.

## *Pause*

Choose one situation where you would like to set a boundary. You can set some others later. I recommend you start with something small and with someone who isn't particularly challenging in your life.

Write down the boundary you would like to set and then think about how you will communicate that boundary, what support you might want or need and when you would like to set that boundary.

---

I recommend not starting with your most difficult relationship. You want to build confidence in your boundary-setting, so start with someone who you think or know will be more receptive to you doing this. You could even role-play with someone you already have good boundaries with. As you proceed, check in with your three circles and see how you're feeling.

This can be a challenging process, and you might find your threat system is feeling activated. If that's your experience, ask yourself what you need in this moment and do your best to give yourself that. Maybe a few soothing breaths will help.

Sometimes, when you're starting to practise something new, it can be great to have some help. This might be from a close friend or family member, a colleague or a more structured support like coaching or therapy. This is another area that a lot of people can struggle with, so let's look at what might be going on if you're someone who struggles to ask for the help you need.

FROM SELF-NEGLECT TO SELF-COMPASSION

## Asking for help and why it can be so hard

Many people struggle to ask for or accept help. Refusing or feeling unable to seek help when you need it can be a result of feeling vulnerable and fearful that you might be rejected, or being judged as incompetent, inadequate or weak. The fear of being a burden to others, or of asking too much or more than you believe you deserve, can be very strong. These fears and beliefs have developed throughout your life and can keep you stuck, isolated and unable to access the support you need.

We're not designed to be solo beings navigating this world by ourselves. It is inbuilt in our DNA that we're social creatures, reliant on the engagement of others for our collective wellbeing. Yet this can feel difficult at times. Allowing yourself to be vulnerable and talk about the struggles you might be having at different times means you need to acknowledge you can't and don't have to do everything by yourself. It also takes willingness to be with any feelings of inadequacy, not being good enough, or being an imposter – yes, most of us experience this at some point, some more frequently than others. I can't tell you how many times thoughts like this have shown up for me whilst writing this book. The process of writing this book has been a journey of continually reconnecting to myself, reaching out for help and offering myself regular doses of compassion. If I had given in to my fears, listened to my self-critic or tried to do everything by myself, I seriously doubt you'd be reading this now.

When you shine a light on what you see as your failings, and depending on the response you receive, this can interfere with pursuing further support when needed. Hopefully, you receive the understanding, kindness and compassionate response that you deserve. Unfortunately, there's still a stigma around seeking help (particularly when it's therapeutic in nature) or even acknowledging our humanness in some circumstances. Maybe it's an unspoken (although sometimes loudly spoken) belief that we 'should' focus on others and leave our own struggles for another time. Whatever it is, it's part of what's clouding the way you relate to yourself, take care of your health and live your life.

What if you could bring your whole self to the conversations you have, or at least those parts of yourself that you would choose to bring? What if you could feel open and vulnerable to speak about what is really happening for you? Maybe it's about your reaction to something or someone in your life. Maybe it's about how you want your work life to look. Maybe it's about how some of your own history is impacting on how you relate to particular people or situations. Maybe it's about acknowledging your neurotype and wanting to talk about how you can best navigate the world. As you start to share more of yourself, you might want to do this slowly and start with the people you already feel safe with before doing this on a broader scale. It is important we take care of ourselves at all times. Unfortunately, we live in a world where not everyone is as accepting as we would like them to be.

How can you seek out other people who provide the necessary sense of safeness? When it comes to finding someone to share your thoughts and feelings with, it could be helpful to consider the following:

- Are you looking for someone in a coaching or therapeutic role or do you want to talk in a more informal way, e.g. with a friend or family member?
- If you want to work with someone in a coaching or therapeutic role, it's important to find someone who works in an

area that fits your relating style and the topics you want to address.
- Do you want to speak to someone about your business or work?
- Is this someone you can feel comfortable with? This will be unique to you.
- Can they meet you at the stage you're at and work to your agenda – not their own?
- Do they demonstrate compassion for others?
- Can they provide you with direction and support?
- Are they non-judgemental?
- Will they respect your cultural needs, religious or spiritual views, gender identity and sexual orientation?

You matter. Your needs are important. You deserve the time and space to explore what you need and want in a relationship that is caring, non-judgemental, compassionate and can provide a sense of safeness. You might need a combination of both structured and informal support. It is not either/or; you need to think about what would be best for you in each context and honour what you need, whilst also being aware of any external or internal barriers you have to seeking that support. There can be many barriers to seeking support. I've given some examples below.

**External barriers to support-seeking can include:**
- Lack of available people or resources
- Cost of accessing support
- Time barriers
- Inaccessible services
- Lack of culturally appropriate services

- Lack of neuro-affirming services
- Lack of LGBTQIA+ friendly services

**Internal barriers to support-seeking can include:**

- Fear of judgement
- Overwhelm and burnout
- Minimising your distress or need
- Feeling unworthy
- History of emotional neglect by others
- Long-term neglect of your own needs
- Fear of reaching out for help and not getting the response you want or need
- Feeling weak/incompetent/less than
- Shame

Think about your own external and internal barriers to seeking support. You might like to write these down as a reminder for when you're struggling to ask for the help you need.

We may fear that by being vulnerable
and showing our true selves,
people may reject us or love us less.

The reality, I have found, is that
when we show up as ourselves,
people love us more.

And when we allow others to truly see us,
it allows them to show themself too.

## Rest as an asset

First, rest will look different for different people. Not everybody has the same requirements for the amount of rest they need, and not everyone enjoys or feels benefit from the same things. You need to think about rest in the sense of what feels restful for your body and mind and restorative for your nervous system so it can return to a more balanced state. Remember those three circles. Now, this is in no way a prescription for what your rest time should look like, merely some things for you to think about and then determine what is right for you. You know yourself better than anyone else ever will, and you know, or are getting to know, your likes and dislikes. If you give yourself the opportunity to tune in and listen to your wisdom, you can learn how much rest you really need, or at least what might be a good amount to start experimenting with. Remember, the amount of rest you need will change depending on the circumstances you're in.

It can be helpful to ask the people in your life, who know you well and care about you, what they think about how you take care of yourself and how much they think you rest. As long as they do this gently, having someone point out your blind spots can be really helpful. It can bring your attention to things you've not noticed in yourself and assist you in making the changes you might need to make. At the end of the day, you don't know what you don't know, and you can't change what you're not aware of.

There are different ways to rest, and it's important to tune in to yourself and ask what you need at different times throughout your day/week/month/year. When you understand what you need, you can start to prioritise rest and take care of your wellbeing. There are many types of rest we can consider: physical, emotional, creative, cognitive, sensory, social and spiritual. Let's explore them separately. I've laid these out randomly, not in any order of importance. I'll give you some suggestions of how you might engage in each type of rest, but please remember, they are merely suggestions, not a prescription for how to do things.

**Physical rest** is important as it allows your body to rest and repair. When you allow yourself to rest physically, you can reduce tiredness and restore energy for other activities you want or need to engage in.

Physical rest might look like:

- Sitting with a cup of tea
- Having a nap
- Going for a sleep
- Having a massage or stretching your body

**Emotional rest** is another important area of rest. It is all too easy to get caught up in the stressors of every day and push away your feelings. Unfortunately, this can contribute to burnout and mental health concerns. Both lead to needing to take time away from the things that matter to you, so taking regular time during your day/week/month/year will be worth it.

Emotional rest might include:

- Honouring your need for alone time
- Identifying and avoiding stressors where possible
- Spending time with supportive people, perhaps a trusted friend, coach or therapist
- Journalling about your feelings and experiences

- Engaging in creative pursuits
- Setting boundaries

It's about finding what works best for you.

**Creative rest** involves stepping away from the constant need to be producing and creating. This can feel challenging when you've been socialised in a capitalist society to believe that productivity means being worthwhile. Constantly being in the pursuit of outcomes is exhausting, so creative rest can be helpful in giving your mind time to rest, daydream and explore new ideas.

It might include:

- Taking a break from work, whether that is short breaks throughout your day or a longer break away from work. Both are valuable.
- Engaging in something purely for the pleasure of it rather than producing an outcome, like immersing yourself in a creative activity you enjoy, such as dancing, painting, drawing, sewing, cooking, etc.

Allowing yourself to get into a flow state and be present to what you are doing can relax your nervous system and help you recharge.

**Cognitive** rest means giving your brain a break and reducing the ongoing stimulation.

This might look like:

- Stopping the scroll and closing down social media for a while

- Putting your phone away so you're not tempted to keep checking it.
- Stopping what you're doing and staring into the distance for a minute or two
- Meditation

A number of guided meditations are available to you throughout this book, or you can find a multitude of them online. Taking these brain breaks can help you stay focused and productive, so they're well worth incorporating into your day. Even a few minutes of slowing down and taking deep in-breaths and nice long out-breaths can make a lot of difference.

**Sensory rest** involves taking a break from all the sensory stimuli that comes your way daily. Noise, light, smells – it's constant and can be overwhelming, particularly if you're neurodivergent like me. Please don't make me go to the grocery store and walk down the laundry aisle. With so many overwhelming smells and bright lights, no thanks.

Ways you can have some sensory rest include:

- Dimming or turning off the lights
- Turning off the television or music, or alternatively, listening to some calming music
- Avoiding places with strong smells
- Having some quiet time in nature
- Taking a bath – this might increase sensory stimulation, so check if this feels restful for you

Taking even a two-minute break and closing your eyes can make a difference in your day.

Let's do a little experiment. You might want to record this on your phone so you can play it back with your eyes closed or read the instructions and then do the practice. It's just a quick one.

> If it feels comfortable to do so, gently close your eyes. Notice how even just that small action of closing your eyes feels different to having your eyes open and taking in all the stimuli around you.
>
> Keeping your eyes closed, look to your left and then to your right, then look up and look down. Repeat these actions three times.
>
> Now allow your eyes to rest. Just allow them to be still. Notice how different it feels when your eyes are rested. Notice how much less energy it takes to have your eyes closed and still.
>
> When our eyes are open, they are constantly scanning and moving all day long. Now, give them a moment to rest. Let them be still.
>
> When you feel ready, you can open your eyes.

This exercise highlights how busy our eyes are every day. Our eyes (and brain) are taking in constant stimuli and continually moving, even when we're not aware that they are. How different did it feel for you when your eyes were moving and when your eyes were still? Just a few moments with closed, still eyes can give you some much-needed rest throughout your day.

Resting your senses can help you avoid sensory overwhelm and ultimately reduce stress. This being said, if you're a neurodivergent person (particularly ADHD), you might find there are times when you feel stressed due to under-stimulation and would benefit from sensory seeking. In this instance, knowing what sensory stimulation is helpful and benefits your wellbeing can help you avoid impulsive sensory-seeking that might actually be harmful to your overall wellbeing.

**Social rest** will look different depending on how draining or energising you find social interaction. It might also depend on the type of social interactions, and you might need to decrease some more than others. We are all social beings, but that doesn't mean you have to follow some social 'norm'. Giving yourself opportunities to recharge your energy is important.

This might look like:

- Declining a social invitation (or a few)
- Keeping your socialising to one-on-one or small groups of close friends and family
- Carving out time to be by yourself
- Taking yourself on a solo date for dinner, the movies or a nice walk.

Be curious about your social needs and how you can maintain boundaries and time for recharging, as well as maintaining connection with others.

**Spiritual rest** allows you to connect more deeply with who you are and how you want to live your one precious life. It isn't about organised religion (although it might be if this is important to you).

It might involve:

- Spending time in nature
- Connecting with Country and ancestors
- Engaging in yoga practice

- Meditating alone or with a group
- Taking on a volunteering role.

## *Pause*

Take a moment to think about the things you like to do to rest. Spend some time writing down a few of those things. We will come back to these later. Also write down the name of the person or people who you could talk to about how you take care of yourself. Remember, choose a person (or people) who you know has your best interests at heart. Being made aware of our blind spots isn't always comfortable and is easier when someone does it in a loving, gentle and caring way.

It can be easy to trick yourself into thinking you're resting when actually you're still busy engaging in activities. I can be really good at this, especially when I have something I'm enjoying that I want to get done, even when I know that I need to rest. You might recognise yourself in some of the following.

How many times do you tell yourself you'll rest and then find yourself picking up your phone and checking emails, socials or reviewing your calendar to see what you have coming up?

How often do you tell yourself you're going to take some time to rest and find that your mind is busy, busy, busy thinking about all the things and then before you know it, you're up and about attending to them?

How often do you tell yourself you're resting when you're watching a thriller, drama or action movie but in reality, you're not resting because your nervous system is on high alert? Now, I'm not saying taking time out to watch your favourite show isn't enjoyable and important, but let's not kid yourself that watching the latest true crime doco is adequately resting your nervous system. When you watch a show, your brain responds to it as though you are watching it in real life. You feel anxious, tense or shocked in the same way you would if the thing that made you anxious, tense or shocked was happening right in front of you. It's all a nervous system response. So, whilst you might find thrillers and dramas enjoyable to watch, you might not want to keep choosing them as your go-to for resting your nervous system.

Rest isn't the only thing you need; you also need activities that are replenishing, and we will get to those soon. It's important that you don't get them mixed up and convince yourself that you're resting when in fact you're not. I know I can be like that at times, and I have to have a chat with myself and remind myself that I'm actually still working or heavily engaged cognitively with something I'm doing. I don't necessarily stop myself from doing these things. I just do my best to do them intentionally, and make sure I'm factoring in rest that is actually restful.

Notice how I say *do my best*, because it's certainly not always easy. You're a human with a tricky brain and holding yourself to standards where you have to do everything perfectly, always live completely in line with your values and never get things wrong, is an unhelpful and impossible way to live. Plus, it's true that you learn more from your mistakes.

So, let's do a quick review of what rest might look like.

Resting might be going somewhere quiet for a nap; having a snooze in the sun; taking some time, even just a few minutes, to close your eyes and block out the immense stimuli you are subjected to every day. It might involve getting an early night a few nights a week so you can give yourself more sleep opportunity. Sleep opportunity is the amount of time you give yourself where sleep is a possibility. If you're aiming for a minimum of eight hours of sleep a night, you have to be in bed for at least eight hours, or you've got no chance. You can't control how much sleep you have each night, but you can choose how much sleep opportunity you give yourself. I speak to many women who struggle with sleep, and one quick tip I give is to tell your mind that you are resting. I heard this at a training by Steve Hayes, co-founder of *Acceptance and Commitment Therapy*. I tried it, and it worked well for me. By telling yourself you're resting, you help avoid your mind trying to solve the problem of not sleeping. Your mind will always try to solve a problem, so if you're telling yourself you can't sleep, then your mind is likely to start worrying about the impact of this, which will in turn make sleep more elusive. If you tell your mind you're resting, then there is nothing to solve. Cool trick, hey!

Rest might involve getting a massage, a sound healing or a session in a float tank. Ooh, yes please – sign me up. It might involve finding a quiet space to lay your body down for a few moments or gently resting in your chair rather than rushing around before your next task.

Many women I speak to book appointments back-to-back for at least part of their day. If this is something you do, it might be worthwhile thinking about how your day is planned out and whether that really works for you. What motivates you to plan your day that way, and how does it feel rushing from one appointment to another? Think about how your day might be different if you gave yourself some breathing space between each appointment or at least between some of them. Perhaps you could trial it and see how it feels and what you prefer. You may also decide that some back-to-back appointments work for you, as it may allow space somewhere else in your day that is more helpful for you. Do what is right for you, but take the time to see if what you're doing is actually right for you and what is motivating your choices.

You might be employed and thinking this level of choice and autonomy isn't available to you, but have you ever thought about speaking to your employer about whether some changes and accommodations can be made for you? There's no guarantee they will agree, but there's no chance of change if you don't have the conversation. You might be a busy parent who barely gets the chance to catch your breath during the day. How could you take some moments amid the chaos?

For many of us, stopping and resting can be tricky, particularly when we are used to being busy and productive. Resting can seem like a waste of time or not as important as all the other things you have to do for yourself and for other people. Resting can bring up a critical inner voice telling you that you're lazy, or you'll never meet your goals if you keep sitting around. Perhaps these are messages you've heard from others and internalised. Resting can in fact feel quite uncomfortable, particularly if it is not something you are used to doing. So, if you choose to rest and your mind starts to tell you that you should be doing something, remind yourself that you are doing something: you're resting. Remind yourself that resting is actually an important part of your day. Resting allows you to refresh. It can help promote your mental and physical health, help reduce stress, improve your mood and actually increase your productivity. So, you can tell your tricky mind this if it's intent on being busy all the time: being busy when tired may not produce the results you're actually looking for.

Try resting for a while and see how different you feel when you re-engage in your tasks or activities. You may need to do this more than once to notice a change, but why not give it a go? Remember, as with anything new, start small and build up from there. Practise being with any discomfort that shows up and over time, you will find it gets easier. You can always return to how you've been doing things if this isn't helpful for you. Experiment for yourself and see.

Sometimes, rest might involve a compromise, such as working under a blanket on the couch. This may give you some level of sensory rest whilst still engaging in the work you need to do. Or, you might be resting your body physically whilst watching a thriller (if that's your genre of choice). There's no one right way. It's about figuring out what works for you. One of the ways I encourage myself to rest is with my *pyjamas-on-purpose days*. These are days when I get up and make an intentional choice to stay in my pyjamas, or shower and get back into some pyjamas. I confess that I have sleeping pyjamas and house pyjamas. This isn't the same as those days where you feel unmotivated and can't be bothered to get dressed. This is an intentional self-care choice. Sometimes, my pyjamas-on-purpose days are filled with rest, relaxation and my favourite show. Other days, I'm cosy in my pyjamas, and I choose to get some work or life admin tasks done, or perhaps some creative writing as I find that very nourishing.

## *Pause*

Take a moment to think about your relationship with rest. Write down the different ways you rest (or if you neglect this, write down what you think other people do to rest). You might like to ask yourself the following questions:

- *What tends to motivate me to rest? (e.g. I'm exhausted and have to stop; someone reminds me to rest; I recognise the value of rest and schedule it into my days)*
- *Do I schedule rest into my calendar/diary? If not, would I consider doing that, and what would it look like? If this isn't something I would consider doing, why not? (By the way, it might not work well for you to do this, and that's totally okay too)*
- *What thoughts, feelings or physical sensations show up when I think about prioritising and taking time for rest?*
- *What do I think might be different for me if I allowed myself to rest?*
- *After reflecting on these questions, how important do I now think rest is for me?*

Rest isn't the only piece of the puzzle, of course, although it is a significant piece. We also need to do things that are nourishing and fill up our cup. So, let's talk about what they might be.

*Rest in the deep flow of your breath
and come home to yourself.*

## Replenishing – you need to pour in too

As I said before, we also need activities that are replenishing, that fill our cup, so to speak. We ideally want our cup full to overflowing so that when we give out to others, it comes from a place of abundance and doesn't deplete us. Replenishing, or engaging in activities that fill your cup, may include busier activities. They are usually the things that invoke feelings like joy, excitement, contentment, pleasure and satisfaction.

For many people, particularly for Autistic folk, engagement in our special interests (SpIns) can be an essential part of our self-care and overall wellbeing. When we engage in these in a helpful way, they can have many benefits, including stress reduction, self-soothing, social connection, a sense of accomplishment and a stronger connection to, and sense of, self. Unfortunately, the dark side of SpIns can be hyper-focus. This can lead to neglecting other areas of your life and wellbeing and can be a contributing factor for burnout. Personally, I set alarms to remind me to take regular breaks when I am sitting down to work on any of my SpIns. I actually set alarms every day, no matter what I'm doing, because I've come to know that having pre-set reminders is really helpful for me.

Replenishing activities might look like:

- Catching up with friends
- Going to a party
- Going to a live music event
- Wandering around your favourite markets
- Exercising or engaging in a fun sport
- Connecting with a cultural practice
- Working on a passion project

- Reading
- Researching a favoured topic
- Engaging in a craft activity
- Playing a musical instrument
- Listening to podcasts (like my podcast *Welcome to Self®* maybe?)

Replenishing activities are just as important as restful activities. It's not one or the other. It's not about choosing to rest *or* replenish. You need both, so you need to be mindful and intentional about what you're doing. You might also find that you have some of the same activities on both lists. Different activities can feel different at different times. I know that for me, watching shows can be a source of restfulness and replenishment, depending on how I'm feeling and what I'm watching.

Being in connection with others can be soothing and healing, and of course, fun. It can also be tiring, exhausting and take time away from other restful activities that your mind and body need. We know as human beings that social connectedness is really important. It's how we're wired, a biological need, and this need will differ between individuals. Again, it's about getting to know yourself so you can have the right amount of connection for you.

Think about the last time someone asked you if you'd like to catch up and you were feeling tired that day. What did you do? Do you have a tendency to automatically say yes because you don't want to let the other person down? Do you fear missing out, or worry there won't be another invitation? Or are you able to give yourself some time to reflect on how you're feeling, what you want and need, and what the consequences of your choice will be?

It gets tricky when you want to both rest and replenish, and they conflict with each other. That's when you need to really think about the outcome of your choices and what would be best for you. When you find yourself in a situation like that, see if there is an alternative. Perhaps you could catch up another time, after you've rested. Maybe there is something you could do together that would be restful for you both. This is when you can use that tricky yet brilliant, creative and compassionate mind to imagine different possibilities. Possibilities that consider your needs and wellbeing. Take the time to bring awareness to what is motivating your decision. Try your best to make a choice in line with your values, from a place of feeling grounded with a calm mind, rather than a decision that merely serves to settle your threat system. Remember, this takes practice. No one manages to do this all of the time. You're a human being with a tricky mind doing the best you can under the circumstances you're in with the knowledge, skills and resources that you have. So, go gently with yourself. Hopefully moving forward, you'll be able to make more informed choices about what you're doing and why.

### *Pause*

Take a moment to look back at your list of your restful activities. Do you still think they are restful? Which of them would you change to replenishing? Write down what you find restful and what you find replenishing.

Because we've been thinking about rest, I invite you to take a few moments now to rest and soothe. You might want to record this on your phone so you can play it back with your eyes closed, or use the QR code and I will guide you.

## A TIME TO REST

*I invite you to find a comfortable position, ideally with your feet on the floor, in an upright position allowing an open diaphragm. You can open your diaphragm by gently rolling your shoulders up and back. Most important is that you listen to what your body needs and give yourself permission to do that. It might be sitting on a chair or the floor, laying down on the floor or your bed, or in any other position that suits you. Honour your body in a way that feels comfortable.*

*Gently close your eyes or rest your gaze in front of you. Now bring your attention to your breath and notice the rhythm and pace of your breath. Notice if it feels shallow and quick, or slow and deep. Take a moment to gently deepen your in-breath and gently lengthen your out-breath. Spend a few moments with yourself resting in the soothing rhythm of your breath.*

*As you do this, notice how your mind and body feel compared to how you were feeling before you started. Really notice what slow feels like, what it feels like to rest. Remember, your mind may wander, and that's perfectly normal. That's what our minds do. You can just notice this and gently bring your attention back to your breath, remembering you might need to do this many times in one sitting.*

> *Now start to notice the sounds around you. Gently guide your attention to how it feels to be sitting or lying where you are. Gently make some small movements with your fingers and toes. Spend some more time resting in the soothing rhythm of your breath.*
>
> *When you feel ready, gently open your eyes and bring your attention back to the environment you're in.*

Allowing yourself to slow down throughout the day, even when your mind is telling you that you have so much to do, can be extremely helpful and make a real difference to your day. Your mind might tell you that you don't have time to slow down, but it could take you less than sixty seconds, and who doesn't have sixty seconds? So, whether you take sixty seconds or sixty minutes or whatever suits you, I hope you can give yourself some time to slow down and rest and notice how it feels when you tend to yourself in this way.

### Maggie's case study

There was a time in my professional life when I completely lost myself.

I was working full time from a therapy room I rented, and I kept adding more and more clients into my calendar. I was focused on meeting my clients' needs and didn't realise the severe impact this was having on my body and energy levels. I was caught up in people-pleasing, managing a large caseload and overworking. I didn't take long enough breaks between clients and would work until late into the evening. I was becoming ill with various throat viruses, gut issues and persistent joint pain. I began to feel more vulnerable as I experienced intense perimenopause symptoms.

I certainly wasn't living life the way I wanted to. My confidence, self-esteem and self-worth plummeted, and I felt so burnt out. I barely recognised the person I had become. It affected everything. Not just my work, but my friendships too. I began to withdraw from them, and I stopped attending the gentle social events I used to love. I felt ashamed, sad and deeply isolated. I remember one conversation where someone simply said, 'You deserve better than this.' That sentence broke through the fog, and for the first time in a long time, I started to choose me.

I met Hayley via a compassion-focused social media hashtag and first joined Hayley's original Welcome to Self® meetings for therapists during the pandemic. This helped me to engage in conversations around self-care with other wonderful, like-minded people. I began to notice how out of balance I had become and that I wasn't alone in this. I saw how my people-pleasing tendencies were getting in the way of my self-compassion. I had the opportunity to develop more *self-awareness around the choices I was making for myself and to look at ways to be more honest with myself about what I was missing and how I needed to take care of myself more effectively. I gained a more realistic sense of what I needed for myself, and the support I received within the group gave me the courage and strength to be more confident to say, 'No' to others, reduce my client caseload and set clearer boundaries for myself.*

*I finally believed in myself more and felt more comfortable calling myself a businesswoman, something I had struggled with and avoided previously. I had a stronger sense of wanting to lean into how I was running my business and what improvements I could continue to make, so I invested in some group business coaching with Hayley. Through my participation in these groups, my network of other compassionate colleagues has continued to grow, and the friendships I have established and maintained from these experiences bring me so much pleasure and joy. I have gained so much more strength and courage to connect more congruently with a community of compassionate others willing to show up authentically, so we can learn from each other's challenges and changes, as well as celebrate each other's wins.*

*I am more confident to reflect openly and honestly and to be vulnerable in front of others. I used to be afraid of speaking out in groups and felt I would be misunderstood and struggle to explain things clearly. I feared people would think I didn't know what I was talking about and was anxious about others discounting what I was saying. I would feel the need to defend myself, and I wouldn't handle differences or conflict well.*

*Developing my wise, compassionate self enables me to live with more acceptance that I can stay on my path and what I choose to do is absolutely good enough for me. Not everyone is going to like me, or agree with me, and that is absolutely okay. Before, I would have described myself as anxious, small and limited. There were days my inner critic shouted that I was failing, but I learnt to talk to that voice with compassion. I'd say things like, 'Thanks for your concern, but I'm choosing a different path.'*

*I began to trust that my intuition had been right all along. One phrase from Hayley's coaching really landed with me: 'My favourite thing about choice is that you can always choose again.' That idea became a lifeline. I didn't have to stick with decisions that no longer served me; I could choose something different, and I did. Now, I feel connected to myself, I trust myself and I genuinely care about myself. This transformation wasn't fast or always easy. It was slow, messy and deeply human. But it was mine, and I wouldn't trade it for anything.*

# *Congratulations, you finished Part III*

## Take a moment to CARE for yourself

### CELEBRATE

Don't forget to celebrate along the way. Even small moments of celebration can make a difference to how we feel.

What is one thing you are proud of yourself for?

How will you celebrate? Be specific about what you'll do and when. You're more likely to do it if you're specific.

Remember, celebrations don't have to be big or elaborate. It's the act of slowing down, acknowledging and celebrating that matters, not what it looks like.

### APPRECIATE

Appreciate where you are at right now.

What is something you are grateful for?

What is something you need to do your best to accept right now?

### REFLECT

What is something you would like to change?

### EXHALE

Take a moment to do ten soothing breaths.

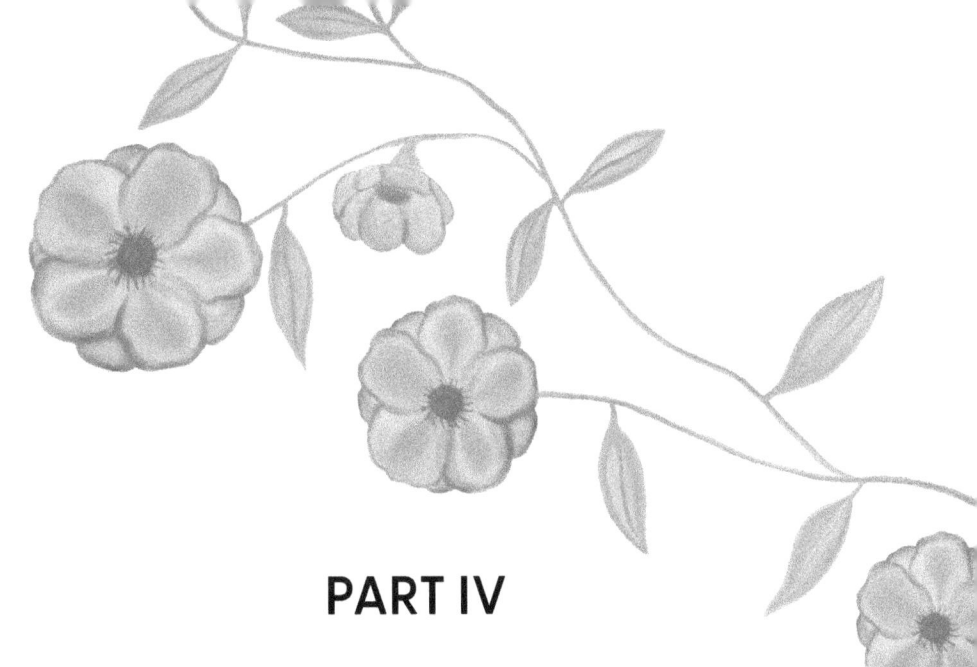

## PART IV

# FINDING YOUR NEW WAY OF BEING

# 10

# *The Parts of Life That Need Your Care*

It's all well and good having new ideas, learning new ways of doing something and thinking how helpful it could be for us, but nothing changes until we put these new learnings into practice. Unfortunately, that's where we can come unstuck.

Our brains love the familiar, the constants. Even if they're not ideal, they can still feel better than the unfamiliar. We can be keen to make changes but find the process of change a real challenge. When we can understand what is happening in these moments, we can draw on our new knowledge to help us with this decision-making.

*Knowledge gives us the power to make change.*

Remember, you have a finely tuned threat system designed to keep you safe. Trying new things is like an invitation to your mind to come up with what I like to call *Freaking Believable Reasons (FBRs)* for why you shouldn't do something. In CFT, FBRs actually stands for Fears, Blocks and Resistances. They show up as inhibitors to your motivation and can be strong when you're learning to be compassionate. We all have these FBRs. As women, we've been socialised to stay small, and not to use our voices. These fears and doubts can take over and you end up being driven by your threat system (red circle).

So, let's look at what these FBRs are, their differences and how they might show up in your life.

**Fears** – These are the what-ifs, the catastrophising and the worst-case scenarios that your tricky brain comes up with when you want to do something new, rest or generally take care of yourself. Think about any fears you have about making changes. They could show up like:

*If I try this new thing, it might go wrong.*
*People might not like me if I start letting them know my boundaries.*
*What if I don't like the changes I make?*
*People will think I'm lazy.*
*I'll become selfish and be like [insert name of person you don't want to be like].*

**Blocks** – These are the things that get in the way and trip you up when you're facing something new. They could be practical elements like:

*I'm really busy and don't have a lot of spare time.*
*I don't have the necessary financial resources.*
*My support for things I need is limited.*
*I have to prioritise others because …*

**Resistances** – Ah, yes, resistance, that pull away from the new, when a part of you wants to stay in the comfort zone (even when it's not all that comfortable).

> I don't believe it will be helpful/work.
> I've tried it before, and nothing changed.
> I just don't want to do it right now.

Now that we have an idea that these *Freaking Believable Reasons* might show up when we want to make changes, it's important we notice them when they do, or we risk letting them drive our decision making.

## *Pause*

I invite you to bring to mind one thing that you would love to change. As you answer the following questions, notice any fears, blocks or resistances that show up for you. They might show up as thoughts, images, feelings or physical sensations.

- What is the one thing I would like to change?
- When would I like to change it?
- What internal resources can I draw on to help me change this?
- What external resources can I draw on to help me change this?
- What fears, blocks and/or resistances do I notice?

## FROM SELF-NEGLECT TO SELF-COMPASSION

Before you move on, I invite you to place your hand on your heart, slow down your breath (remember the soothing breathing we did earlier) and take a moment to connect to the part of you that is wise, strong, courageous and caring; the compassionate part of you that wants the best for you. The part of you that knows your history, your struggles and your fears. The part of you that wants to be helpful and supportive. The part of you that wants the best for you.

There's such a difference in the way you speak and act when the fears are upfront. Once this changes, there's belief and trust in yourself. You can become more curious and expansive. When you can connect with the compassionate part of yourself, it gives you strength and courage. You can access your wisdom. You can make choices that mean you're creating the life you want to have and, in my opinion, that's absolutely beautiful and no less than you deserve. If you can keep coming back to yourself and connecting with your compassionate self, this is going to help you move forward on the things you want to do; the calls you've got to make; the email you've got to write to somebody; the 'Yes' you want to say to an opportunity, or the 'No' you need to say to somebody because it doesn't align with you.

Attending to your wellbeing may seem like common sense, and yet it can be one of the first things that takes a back seat when you need it most. When thinking about your wellbeing, you will benefit most from a holistic approach. Think about *all* the areas in your life that require your care and attention. Self-care looks different for each of us. You have different preferences, and these preferences may change at different times. You also have different access and opportunities for engaging in certain activities due to your own finances, health, life circumstances, etc. Let's think about the different domains in life that build up your overall wellbeing and how you might tend to these for yourself through compassionate care and attention.

We'll look at eight domains – emotional, cultural, spiritual, social, intellectual, physical, financial and occupational. The more you know yourself and reflect on how you can take care of yourself, the more you can create the life you want and allow yourself to thrive. Remember, there is no prescription here. Find things that feel right for you and have a few ideas to choose from.

## Emotional

Your emotional wellbeing matters, and there are many things you can do to support yourself emotionally.

Some ideas to consider for your emotional wellbeing include:

- Listening to music
- Talking to a trusted friend
- Watching something that suits the mood you are in, or something that can shift your mood (e.g. watching a comedy if you are feeling flat)
- Going for a walk or doing a yoga class (there are lots online if you can't leave the house)
- Engaging in something creative like painting, drawing or writing poetry
- Hugging someone you care about
- Laughing with a friend
- Crying and feeling the release of the emotion you have been holding in
- Finding healthy ways to express your frustrations and anger
- Journalling and expressing yourself through writing
- Dancing

Think about some things you can do for your emotional wellbeing and write them down.

## Cultural

Staying connected to your culture can be an important aspect of your wellbeing if it allows you to feel a sense of belonging and connectedness. It can help you to understand aspects of your life, beliefs and ways of being in the world. Being connected to your culture allows you to understand your worldviews as well as understanding the differences of others. It allows you to better understand your own identity and know yourself more. The more you know yourself, the better you can take care of yourself.

Some ways you might connect to your culture may be to:

- Visit places of cultural significance
- Talk to Elders in your community
- Cook cultural dishes
- Read books
- Watch theatre, dance or television performances
- Connect with others in your community
- Speak to family members
- Share about your culture with someone from a different culture

Think about what you can do for your cultural wellbeing and write these down. Notice how you feel when you think about connecting with your culture.

## Spiritual

I admire the wisdom and gentleness that shows through in Maya Angelou's words. I particularly like her words from '*Try to be a rainbow in someone else's clouds'* where she says, 'Someone who may not call God the same name as you, if they call God at all'. For me, this speaks to such acceptance that not everyone thinks the same or believes in the same things. Your spirituality is whatever it means to you, and it can be an important part of your overall wellbeing.

Some ways you might nurture this aspect of your life may be through:

- Meditation
- Visiting a significant and meaningful site
- Being out in nature
- Prayer
- Engaging in yoga
- Considering the meaning and purpose of your life
- Considering what you can do to be of service and support to others
- Loving your fellow humans and animals
- Helping those in need.

Think about what spirituality means to you and how you can support your spiritual wellbeing. Write these down.

## Social

Taking care of your social wellbeing is important, and this will differ in terms of how much social connection you desire or need. You might thrive on lots of social connection, or you might enjoy more solitude with small bursts of connection with others. Whatever is right for you is what matters. You might want to pay attention to how you feel in different social situations and when you have time alone, and see how you feel in terms of energy, joy, desire, etc.

Some of the ways you can take care of your social wellbeing may be to:

- Meet up with friends and family (in person or online)
- Engage in healthy and enjoyable social media use
- Have a laugh with others
- Reach out to old friendships that have been neglected
- Play games with others (in person or online)
- Connect with like-minded others (in person or online)

Think about your favourite ways of connecting socially and write them down. We all differ so much in the amount of social contact that works for us, so don't worry about what other people are doing.

### Intellectual

Another area of wellbeing that we don't always think about is intellectual stimulation. We have minds that are designed for thinking and have an in-built curiosity about the world around us. Think about a child who constantly asks, 'Why is this?' and 'Why is that?' Time spent putting your curious mind to work thinking about you, your life and how you can best take care of yourself can be really beneficial.

Some of the ways you might take care of your intellectual wellbeing may include:

- Reading a book
- Listening to an audiobook or podcast
- Doing some journaling around your values, hopes, dreams and goals
- Being curious about what is around you

- Completing a jigsaw puzzle
- Trying to learn a new skill
- Taking an online class
- Watching a documentary
- Having a stimulating conversation with a friend
- Learning about some else's perspective

Please remember that there is a lot of pressure in the world for us to be productive. Intellectual stimulation is only one piece of the wellbeing puzzle, and this is about focusing on self-care, not on 'doing all the things'. Think about what you might like to engage in to nurture your intellectual wellbeing and write it down. Go gently with yourself and enjoy any intellectual pursuits you might want to engage in.

**Physical**

Your physical wellbeing is important for the daily functioning of your body, no matter what you look like or what size or shape you are. It's important to consider your own abilities when it comes to your physical health. We live in a world that has a very ableist frame of reference, and depending on your own levels of (dis)ability, this can feel shaming and marginalising. Be compassionate to yourself and work within the limits that suit you and your individual circumstances.

Regular exercise or movement can be helpful in service of your overall health and bone strength. You might need to adapt certain exercises to suit your unique circumstances. When my health was at its worst, movement often looked like reaching my arms above my head a few times or laying on my back moving my legs from side to side. Now I see an exercise physiologist twice a week, focusing on strength-building and cardio, and do my best to go for regular walks and swims. Finding practitioners/health professionals who are compassionate, well-trained and can adapt to your needs can be really helpful.

Some ways of taking care of your physical wellbeing might be:

- Go on regular walks
- Find an exercise routine that suits your lifestyle
- Eat nutritious food
- Drink plenty of water
- See your doctor when you are feeling unwell
- Have regular health check-ups
- Take any prescribed medication you need
- Engage in sexual activities alone or consensually with another person

More ideas might be:

- Stretch your body
- Avoid or minimise alcohol use
- Give yourself adequate sleep opportunity
- Practise relaxation and meditation
- Take regular rest breaks for your body and brain

If you can find some activities that you'll enjoy, you're more likely to engage in them. Some days, you might need to remind yourself it is about willingness, not motivation. For example, are you willing to engage in regular exercise even when you're not feeling motivated? Some days the answer may be yes, and some days you might end up saying no. Whatever the answer, go gently with yourself.

Think about some things you could start doing, get back into doing, or increase/decrease the amount of for your physical wellbeing and write them down. Watch out for any self-criticism that shows up during this exercise, no pun intended! Remember, having a few ideas you can choose from can be helpful, and you don't have to do them all at once.

## Financial

Finances can be a tricky thing for people for all sorts of reasons, including your own family of origin circumstances, the messaging you received whilst growing up, your current relationship with money or the societal messaging you have been exposed to. Finances, however, are another important area of your wellbeing. Inadequate finances or difficulties managing finances can cause a great deal of stress for many people. I must point out that this is in no way financial advice. If this is something you struggle with, I suggest you talk to someone qualified in this area. There are some different things you can do to try to take care of your financial wellbeing. These are just some of my suggestions, things I have found helpful to think about over the years. Money management was something I had to pay close attention to during my thirteen years as a single parent.

- Look at cutting back on unnecessary spending
- Consider what you can borrow instead of buy – this is better for the environment too, so win-win
- Prepare a budget so you are aware of your finances
- Try approaching your service providers to see if you can get better deals
- Cancel subscriptions you no longer use; we can end up with so many of those!
- If you're a business owner, consider where you can cut back on business items and bills

- Look at what you are charging for your services and consider your fee structure

As always, choose what works for you in your individual circumstances. Think about some things you can do for your financial wellbeing and write them down. Notice any fears, blocks and resistances that show up when you think about money and/or charging for your services.

## Occupational

How can you take care of your occupational needs? So often you can find yourself just taking the next expected step, following the path that has been laid out for you. You can be so caught up in the busy and the achieving that you don't always stop to reflect on where you have come from or where you really want to be heading. If you don't want that for yourself anymore, you'll need to consider the changes you want to make to your business or work role to turn it into something you really want to be doing. Something that fits the lifestyle you want to live and something that feels meaningful and enjoyable to you as well. I love helping women do this.

It takes time and energy to reflect on what you're doing and to be honest with yourself about what you enjoy, what you want to keep and what you want to change. It requires you to be vulnerable. If you struggle to think about things you enjoy about your work, it doesn't mean you have to change absolutely everything you do, although it might. Just allow yourself to be curious. You might decide that what you are doing isn't your dream, but someone else's or that you've got new interests. Life may have changed, and the way you work can no longer be accommodated. It can just be about giving yourself time to think about your work in terms of the tasks you do, the way you do them, the hours you work and the environment you work in. Think about the aspects of your work that you do like and figure out how you could do more of those things. On the flip side, what are the aspects of your work that you don't like? Are there ways you can do less of that? Can you outsource or delegate some of the things you'd rather not do, so you can focus on the aspects of your work that you do enjoy?

Think about some things you can do for your occupational well-being? Just let your mind bring up ideas without getting caught up in whether they are practical at this stage. Write them down. You can refine what's workable later.

\*\*\*

Now that we've looked at these domains separately, let's look at them in relation to your life as a whole. As you think about all the different life domains that require your attention, it can be helpful to think about how much time you give to each area. You can think about this in terms of time over a day, week or month; whatever feels most appropriate and helpful for you. You might like to spend some time writing down your thoughts.

Think about whether there are any domains that you would like to give more of your attention to. If there are, what would you like to do differently? For example, you might want to spend more time socialising with friends, adding in a gentle walk a few times a week or perhaps spending more time in nature. I've heard from one of my clients, Maggie, that silent discos in the woods are great fun. Sounds like a great way to connect with nature, yourself and others whilst getting in some exercise.

There are various domains that require your attention. Just pick one or two areas of your life that you know could do with some extra care and nurturance and start slowly. It's important you take care of yourself in the process and give yourself the best chance of making the changes you think will be helpful. As you think about the different areas of your life and those that perhaps you're neglecting, pay attention to what shows up for you. Notice your thoughts, feelings and any physical sensations that may be present and don't forget to watch out for those *Freaking Believable Reasons*.

If there are any blocks or resistances in the way of attending to areas of your life, alongside fears that show up or old stories, bring a gentle curiosity to whatever arises, knowing that you don't have to have it all figured out right now.

### Natasha's case study

*The mid-2000s saw me move to a new country, give birth to my second child, start my private practice, end my long-term relationship and become a solo parent.*

*I experienced significant growth in my private practice at precisely the time when I was the least able to cope with the extra pressure. Looking back, it's no wonder I was struggling to function effectively at the time.*

*I was exhausted and felt like a failure in my business. My calendar was full and I had a waitlist of people wanting to work with me, but I was drowning in admin. I felt overwhelmed by requests for my help. I was working so hard, had built a great reputation but had little money to show for it all. I was owed thousands in unpaid fees and kept making mistakes with my billing. My coach at the time suggested that managing the finances of my business wasn't my forte and I shouldn't do it.*

*I felt like my business had become a monster that kept wanting more and more from me. At the same time, I was being offered opportunities that could take me in positive directions, but I was stuck in overwhelm and uncertainty about what direction to take. I was told to 'get out of my own way'. I wasn't exactly sure what that meant, but I certainly seemed to spend a lot of time worrying about what I needed to do, rather than actually doing it.*

*There weren't enough hours in the day for work and fun, whilst being a part-time single mum. I'd fritter away the spare hours that I had feeling sorry for myself, overwhelmed and exhausted. I continually felt unwell. I found myself in a cycle of being enthusiastic and 'on' for my clients but exhausted and depleted at home. My clients were getting the best of me.*

*So many feelings arose for me, mainly shame, embarrassment and self-criticism. How could I have allowed myself to get into such a mess? I remembered my mother's words from childhood. Perhaps she was right when she muttered under her breath that I was stupid and had no common sense.*

*I still feel the sting of my mother's words decades later, but I now have more skills to soothe myself with the balm of self-compassion and acceptance. Rather than criticise and resent the overwhelmed and burnt out past me, I try to remember that she was just trying to do the best with what she knew at the time.*

*My survival strategy of keeping going, pleasing others and trying to do it all by myself had always worked in the past. How was I to know that this was not sustainable indefinitely?*

*In 2019, already clearly burnt out, I wasn't well resourced to cope with further stressful events: COVID, traumatic client deaths, sexual boundary violations, the death of my mother and the ending of another romantic relationship.*

*I have not been alone on my healing journey. I've been fortunate to have been taught helpful skills and strategies through the support and guidance of some wonderful women who are generous in sharing their own experiences and vulnerability.*

*I am especially grateful for Hayley and her Time to Thrive program. With Hayley's guidance, I am practising what I preach more often. I'm prioritising my own needs, being clear about my boundaries, saying no and risking not being liked by people. I have restructured my work calendar in a way that suits me and enables me the time and space to tend to my own mental and physical health needs.*

*I consistently remind myself that my worth does not lie in my productivity or my ability to please others. It hasn't been a quick* fix for me, and I've been resistant to changing at times. Exercising self-compassion hasn't come easy to me, and it still feels like flexing an unfamiliar muscle. I feel clumsy, and I forget how to do it 'properly'. I then remind myself that there is no 'proper way'. It's my journey, and making decisions in alignment with my personal values is a good place to start.

Creativity is one of my values and guiding principles, along with simplicity and connection. It's no coincidence that when I reflect on my healing journey from burnout to self-compassion, I think of words usually associated with sewing and knitting. I talk about 'unravelling', 'becoming undone', and the need to 'detangle' the mess that years of poor self-care and poor boundaries had created. Creativity in conjunction with self-compassion is helping me heal and come back to myself again and again. I am actively creating a vibrant life that I love through gently undoing and detangling the old one that was slowly destroying me.

*Meet yourself where you are and go from there.
Maybe today you just need to slow down and rest.
Give yourself permission to do what
is right for you in this moment.*

# 11

# *Coming Home to Your Compassionate Self*

Every time you connect with yourself, you strengthen the relationship you have with you. So don't be afraid to check in with yourself regularly. I start each morning by greeting myself with a friendly voice and asking how I feel and what I need for my day ahead. It sounds something like this: 'Good morning, darling, did you sleep well? How are you feeling? What have you got on today? Is there anything extra you need today? I love you.' Now, this might feel silly at first – it did for me – but I invite you to try it and see if it makes a difference.

If I have a big event coming up or I'm heading into a busier season, I do what I call *front loading self-care*. This is when I do my usual check in with myself and then think about what else would be helpful to add in prior to whatever is happening. For example, I might plan some early nights in the lead up or make extra effort to stay hydrated and ensure my nutrition is good. I might factor in more time by myself so I'm not over-stimulated. Whatever it is that feels helpful in ensuring I am as resilient and resourced as I can be before heading into the event or busy period. It's not just about taking care of myself during these times and engaging in recovery after but also knowing that I've set myself up well beforehand. In my experience this has meant it feels easier during and takes less to recover after.

We'll begin this final chapter with another gentle moment of connection; an opportunity to tune in to how it feels when you choose you. Let's take a few quiet moments to gently connect with the compassionate part of you that sees you clearly, without judgement. This is an invitation for you to pause, listen inward, and meet yourself with care. There's no right or wrong way to experience it. Just allow your experience to be whatever it is, and notice what arises. You might want to record this meditation on your phone so you can play it back with your eyes closed, or use the QR code and I will guide you.

## CHOOSING YOU

*I invite you to find a comfortable position, ideally with your feet on the floor, in an upright position allowing an open diaphragm. You can open your diaphragm by gently rolling your shoulders up and back. Most important is that you listen to what your body needs and give yourself permission to do* that. It might be sitting on a chair or the floor, laying down on the floor or your bed, or in any other position that suits you. Honour your body in a way that feels comfortable. Just take a moment to notice how it feels to be where you are and make any micro-movements your body might need.

Notice the sounds around you, listening for the sound farthest away. Now the sound closest to you. Gently bring your attention to the tip of your nose, just starting to notice the in-breath and the out-breath. Just knowing that when you're breathing in, you're breathing in, and when you're breathing out, you're breathing out.

I invite you to gently slow down your breath, focusing on the pace and the rhythm of your breath. Breathe deep into your belly, equal, soothing in- and out-breaths. Just allow yourself to be with yourself. Notice how you feel in this moment. Notice any thoughts that show up in your mind, and as best you can, bring a gentle curiosity to the thoughts, just observing them, not needing to do anything with them.

Spend some time thinking about how it feels when you choose yourself; when you prioritise yourself over other people; when you choose rest over activities; when you choose to say no to others, so you can say yes to yourself.

As you think about these things, notice your breath. Notice if it slows or quickens. Slow it down if needed and notice any thoughts, feelings or physical sensations that start to show up. Notice any discomfort. I know choosing yourself can be difficult.

Now I invite you to connect to the part of yourself that has the intention to be helpful, not harmful; the part of you that knows your history, your experiences and understands your *suffering. The part of you that wants the best for you. The wise, strong, courageous, caring part of you.*

*If it feels helpful, just place a hand over your heart and gently slow down your breath.*

*Now I invite you to gently turn inward to yourself and ask yourself the following questions.*

*Where in my life would it be helpful to choose myself?*

*What do I need in those moments of discomfort when I choose myself?*

*What would be helpful to support me in practising choosing myself?*

*Spend a few more moments in the soothing rhythm of your breath, just noticing your in-breath and your out-breath.*

*As you go through your day, as best you can, hold your intention to be helpful, not harmful. Remember, you can slow down and connect to the wise, strong, courageous and caring part of yourself at any time. The more you practise this, the easier it will become. Your compassionate self is always here waiting for you and ready to support you.*

*Now start to notice the sounds around you. Notice how it feels to be you in this moment. Notice the points of contact between you and where you are sitting or lying. Gently make some small movements with your fingers and toes. As you feel ready, you can open your eyes, bring your attention back to the place you are in and stretch your body or give your body whatever it needs right now.*

Now you've had another opportunity to connect to your compassionate self, I invite you to think about any fears, blocks and resistances you have about choosing yourself and making the changes you want in your life. Once you've thought about these, think about what your compassionate self would say to you. You might want to write these down as a reminder.

You read about compassion, and your compassionate self, earlier in the book and you've just had some more opportunity to connect with that wise, strong, courageous and caring part of you, so let's talk about setting yourself up for success as you move forward.

You've thought about what you want in the different domains of your life and what you can do in each to take care of yourself. You've also learnt about some new ways of being that you can practise. So, what do you want to do with this one precious life you've been gifted?

When embarking on something new, it can be helpful to think about previous changes you've made. Think about challenges you've faced or goals you've set for yourself and achieved. How did you manage to do that? Remember what internal and external resources you drew upon to help you. Perhaps you reached out to someone for assistance. Maybe you trusted your decision-making, made a plan and wrote down your goals, accessed your courage, or offered yourself the self-compassion you deserved. Remember what it felt like when you overcame that challenge or reached your goal. Maybe you doubted you could and then surprised yourself.

When thinking about the changes you'd like to make next, be mindful of not overwhelming yourself. It can be helpful to aim for between one and three new goals. If you're someone who likes to set and achieve lots of goals, you can still do that, but I suggest you set them out up to three at a time and once you've done those, then you can repeat that process as many times as you like. Of course, if you already know that doing it differently to this works well for you, please do it the way it works for you. I'm not here to tell you how to live your life or what to do. I'm merely offering suggestions. So, take what is helpful and leave the rest on the pages of this book. By the way, if you're someone who is turned off by the word 'goals', please change it to a word that you prefer to use. I don't want a five-letter word getting in the way of you living your best life.

Goal-setting might be one of those times when your tricky mind starts jumping in with all sorts of doubts and reasons why you can't do something. Remember, this is how the tricky mind operates, so rather than be surprised, you can expect it and remind yourself that this is how your mind works. You can still move forward despite what your mind is telling you. The following brief exercise helps us realise that we can act in ways that our mind tells us we can't. I invite you to give it a go.

> If you're not near a wall, move closer to one. Now, I want you to say to yourself, 'I can't touch the wall with my hand'. Keep saying this on repeat and at the same time, reach out and touch the wall with your hand.

> Did you do it? Can you see how it's you and not your mind that has control over your actions? Next time your tricky mind tells you that you can't do something, go ahead and see if you can.

When you spend time reflecting on where you've come from and what you've overcome, rather than just where you want to be and what you want to do, it can help you see your strengths and capabilities and help motivate you for your next steps.

## Small steps will get you there

You don't have to take giant leaps to change your life. A series of small, manageable steps not only makes changes but also keeps you from overwhelming your nervous system. You want something to feel doable, not like a mountain you must climb. With that in mind, think about one small thing that you would like to do next that is different to how you have been living your life? Choose something that you know you can achieve; you want to get some wins on the board so you can celebrate and feel motivated to continue to make changes.

When thinking about your next small step, be as specific as you can. Think about what you would like to do, when you would like to do it, what you will need to achieve it and how you will keep yourself accountable. For example, I am going to sit down and have fifteen minutes to myself (what) enjoying a nice cup of lemongrass and ginger tea (what I'll need) before my next meeting/school pick up (when) and I am going to set my alarm to remind me (accountability).

Being specific in terms of what and when, as well as knowing what you need in terms of internal and/or external resources, increases the likelihood of you taking action. Including ways to keep yourself accountable, such as setting alarms or messaging a friend to let them know your intention, can help you feel supported in the process. My present self is often thanking my past self for helping to set me up for success. It can also be helpful to think about any challenges you see getting in the way of doing what you plan to do. You might realise there are aspects of your environment, mindset, health, finances or other practicalities that need your attention in order for you to progress. Finally, consider how confident you feel in being able to offer compassion to yourself as and when needed. You might like to write down some compassionate phrases that you can say to yourself regularly. It can then be helpful to keep these somewhere visible as a gentle reminder to offer yourself compassion.

Allow yourself to dream and set goals and remember, this is your one precious life. These are your dreams and goals. They can be whatever you want them to be. Please do your best not to let anyone, including your sneaky self-critic, tell you that you can't or shouldn't aim for them.

\*\*\*

If you would like to do some more goal setting straight away and would like some guidance, you can access a resource using the QR code below. Alternatively, you might like to take some time to reflect on everything you've read so far and to rest a little before taking your next steps. Whatever you choose, do your best to make it an intentional choice that honours you and your wellbeing.

*You don't need to dim your light for anyone.
If someone doesn't like your brightness,
they can choose to put their sunglasses on.
Be courageously, wholeheartedly You!*

# 12

# *Go Gently with Yourself*

You have explored the emotions and the beliefs you have been holding about yourself and have had the opportunity to reflect on whether these have been helpful for you. If you're anything like me, I'm sure you've realised that some of what you've been believing and telling yourself, and some of the choices you've made, whilst understandable given your life circumstances and experiences, haven't been very helpful. Hopefully, now you've had time to be with yourself, you can see that there is a different way. A way to treat yourself that is more nurturing, loving and compassionate. A way to live your life that allows you to take care of yourself, not just others. A way that allows you to create a life based around your values and desires.

These changes don't happen overnight but are a powerful step to a different way of being with yourself and creating a life that feels meaningful to you. Change comes from taking continued action, not just learning new information, so before we part ways, think about small actions you can do regularly to continue taking care of yourself and making the changes you want. Things you'd like to do daily, weekly and monthly. Having an idea of what you'd like to do to honour your wellbeing or how you'd like to be living your life doesn't automatically mean you'll stick to doing what's necessary, even if you know it'll be helpful. Life circumstances will sometimes get in the way; your tricky mind will continue to be tricky, and at times you might need to prioritise something else over what you were planning to do. That's okay. You can keep coming back to what you want and starting over. The key is to remember to be compassionate to yourself when you go off track and to be compassionate to yourself when you forget to be compassionate to yourself!

I hope this time and space to be reflective and thoughtful about yourself, and your life has been beneficial. I suggest you look back on the reflections and exercises you have completed here and use them as a gift to understand yourself better and to remind yourself that you matter so very much. Above all else, please take some time to acknowledge the gift you have given yourself. The gift of understanding and compassion, of allowing yourself to be curious and open to the possibility of living your life differently. Living in a way that feels aligned, joyful, exciting and free of unnecessary obligation and old patterns that no longer serve you. Celebrate what you have done here, the realisations you had, the limiting beliefs you have disrupted, the values you have connected with, the practices you have engaged in and the choice you have made to treat yourself differently. That is all worth celebrating. Please know I am here celebrating you too.

I encourage you to continue to ask questions of yourself. Be curious and open to hearing the wisdom you hold inside of you. Remember that you are a beautiful, wise, worthwhile human being, and please go gently with yourself.

I'd like to leave you with one final meditation. I wrote this for myself many years ago and share it often at trainings and workshops I present. I hope you find it helpful. You might want to record this on your phone so you can play it back with your eyes closed, or use the QR code and I will guide you.

## RELATIONSHIP WITH YOURSELF

*I invite you to sit in a comfortable upright position with your feet flat on the floor and your hands laying gently in your lap. Or, choose a position that honours your body. Choose a nice open posture and relax your shoulders. Now take a moment to notice how you are sitting or laying and make any adjustments you might need.*

*Gently close your eyes or, if you prefer, gently rest your gaze at a spot in front of you. Take a moment to bring your attention to your breath. Notice that when you are breathing in, you are breathing in and when you are breathing out, you are breathing out. Just allow your breath to find its own soothing rhythm of equal in- and out-breaths.*

*Now I invite you to bring to mind that feeling you get when you are with someone you truly care about. Think about how you listen attentively to what they say. You don't dismiss* them. You're happy to meet their needs in areas that you are capable of. You enjoy spending time with them. When you look at them, it makes you smile. You can see past their individual flaws and appreciate them as a whole person. You want the best for them; for them to be happy, healthy, peaceful and free from harm.

Now imagine feeling that same way about yourself. Wanting to meet the needs that you have, engaging in things that promote your health, happiness and peace. Being able to accept all parts of yourself, even those parts you'd rather avoid.

Imagine if the most beautiful relationship you could ever have was the one you have with yourself. You know yourself better than anyone else in this world. You will spend more time with yourself than anyone else you will ever meet. You will be with yourself at all times in everything that you do. What do you want that relationship to be like?

Now bring to mind the fact that we are all human beings. We all suffer; it is universal. No one escapes it; it is part of being who we are. We love, we cry, we excel, we fall, we stumble and struggle; we stand tall. The temptation can be to wear a mask that tells the world, and ourselves, that, 'I am okay, really I am' even when we are hurting and afraid and ashamed. If we do wear that mask, no one really knows how we feel or what we might need. We even lose sight of it ourselves.

Imagine for a moment, you could take off that mask and be seen for who you are and what you need. Even if you only remove the mask for yourself to start with so you can really listen to what you need and take steps to take care of *yourself. If you could be with yourself in the way you would be with a loved one, someone you deeply care about.*

*And breathe ...*

*Take a few more moments to be with your breath, knowing that when you are breathing in, you are breathing in and when you are breathing out, you are breathing out.*

*Now I invite you to notice how it feels to be sitting or lying where you are. Notice the sounds around you and the temperature of the air on your skin. Start to make some gentle movements with your fingers and toes. As you feel ready, you can open your eyes, bring your attention back to the place you are in and stretch your body or give your body whatever it needs right now.*

## *Welcome to Self*®
*May you go well and go gently with yourself*

# *Congratulations, you've completed the final Part*

## Take a moment to CARE for yourself

**CELEBRATE**

Don't forget to celebrate along the way. Even small moments of celebration can make a difference to how we feel.

What is one thing you are proud of yourself for?

How will you celebrate? Be specific about what you'll do and when. You're more likely to do it if you're specific.

Remember, celebrations don't have to be big or elaborate. It's the act of slowing down, acknowledging and celebrating that matters, not what it looks like.

**APPRECIATE**

Appreciate where you are at right now.

What is something you are grateful for?

What is something you need to do your best to accept right now?

**REFLECT**

What is something you would like to change?

**EXHALE**

Take a moment to do ten soothing breaths.

*Asking for help isn't weak,
it is a sign of great courage
and a commitment
to the reduction of suffering.*

**I choose** to live life out loud.
I will no longer keep myself
small for the sake of others.

I will recognise myself as the
**courageous, beautiful, smart**
woman that I am and I will **offer my**
gifts to the world, as and when I **choose** to do
this. I will not let fear and self-doubt be my guide.

I will tune in and listen to my own **wisdom** before seeking the opinion of others. I will **trust** in my wisdom when she reminds me to reach out to others and **seek their wisdom**.

I will give myself **permission** to embrace the things that feed me, nurture me and remind me that **I am woman**, and **I am worthy**.

I will learn to understand my tricky mind and understand that I have the **power** to make **choices** in my life. I will recognise that the choices available to me may not always be what I want but I will always have a choice. I will recognise that even when I choose not to make a choice, I am in fact making a choice.

I will stand tall, **breathe** and step out into my life as the **owner** of my life.

I will **go gently** with myself, and I will be **assertive** as needed, understanding that gentle does not mean submissive.

I will live with the **intention** to be helpful, not harmful, to myself, others and the earth that supports me.

# *Recommended Reading*

Gilbert, P. (2009). *The Compassionate Mind.* Little, Brown Book Group.

Gilbert, P., & Choden. (2013). *Mindful Compassion.* Robinson.

Irons, C. & Beaumont, E. (2017). *The Compassionate Mind Workbook: A Step-by-Step Guide to Developing Your Compassionate Self.* Robinson.

*Acknowledgements*

Gratitude is an important value for me, so I relish the opportunity to thank the many people who have been pivotal in bringing this book to life. Writing a book is a collective process and whilst it has been me sitting at the computer and typing the words, it is only because of the many people around me that this is even possible. Without the interactions and experiences I have had in my own life, the highly rewarding, the challenging, and everything in between, this book would not exist. Throughout this process, I have been assisted, challenged, and encouraged by so many people, and I am so grateful to them all. I would also like to make special mention of some of those people.

To my publisher Natasha Gilmour, and The Kind Press team. Natasha, your enthusiasm from the start about my book has been delightful. Having you alongside me in this process has felt so supportive and has definitely helped me shape this into something I feel proud to send out into the world. Thank you so much, I wouldn't have wanted to do it without your compassionate and heartwarming support. To Rananda, receiving your editorial feedback about my book did something for me as a writer that I will never forget. It allowed me to see my ability in a new way and boosted my confidence in calling myself an author. Thank you for tightening up my words without changing them and for the beautiful praise you shared. This book is better because of the input of everyone involved in the publishing process.

To Gráinne, thank you for saying yes and joining me in this creative process of bringing to life the vision for my book cover. I love it! Thank you for your patience as I worked out how to express my vision in coherent creative terms. Being a client of Studio Grá has been such a pleasure, and to have the artwork of such a dear friend gracing the cover feels so special to me. I will always treasure this experience we've had together.

Thank you Nyssa, Nyssa Ray Recordings, my dear friend and audio producer. Thank you so much for helping me create the meditations for the book, you added so much joy and fun to the process. Thanks too for all the work you've done on the Welcome to Self® podcast from the beginning. I deeply appreciate you and working with you is always such a pleasure.

I am so grateful to the women who have generously shared their time and stories with me. When I asked each of them their reason for sharing their story, they all spoke to the gratitude they felt for the support they have received during their struggles. They also spoke of their desire to help others feel less alone and inspired that change can happen. Maria, Rebecca, Maggie and Natasha, thank you so much for your honesty, vulnerability and compassion for yourself and others. I have no doubt readers will find inspiration and hope in your words. Thank you to May for giving me permission to share about your experience, you're a remarkable woman and I'm excited to see how life unfolds for you.

## ACKNOWLEDGEMENTS

I extend my deep gratitude to all my current clients, and previous psychology clients. You have trusted me with a part of your lives and businesses, and I don't take that lightly. I have learnt so much from each of you, about myself, the human experience, the capacity to change, and what it means to truly take care of yourself and the consequences if you don't.

Thank you to Professor Paul Gilbert OBE, my teacher, mentor and friend. Thank you for dedicating so much of your life to developing Compassion Focused Therapy and showing me there is a different way to relate to myself. It has changed my life in the most beautiful and powerful ways. Thank you, Paul, for believing in me before I believed in myself, and for encouraging me years ago to share my knowledge and teach others. Respect, love and thanks to you and your beautiful family.

Stacey and the team from Maple & Sage, thank you so much for providing me with such a beautiful and inspiring workspace when I first started my writing journey. Your excitement about a book being created upstairs helped motivate me when my inspiration was low, and of course, the beautiful food helped. Whilst I never got to finish my writing there, and this book is not the one that was started, Maple & Sage is held dear within my writing heart. Stacey, continuing to have you with me each week as my body double, you creating nourishing food and me writing this book, as we listened to favourite playlists, will always be one of my fondest memories. Love you. Oh yeah, and thanks for being my disaster buddy through non-eventful cyclones and earthquakes!

I have been so fortunate to have encouragement, support and wisdom from many dear friends, reminding me, when I forgot, that life comes in seasons and not everything has to happen straight away, no matter how much a part of me might have wanted that. My special thanks go to Rebecca Weiner, Lisa Walton, Emily Wilkinson, Nyssa Ray, Gráinne Schäfer, Jess Spendlove, Peita Mages, Caitlin Bell and Deanne Blackman, thank you. You have all in your own ways helped me stay motivated and focused on the reason I wanted to bring this book to life. Your belief in me and your encouragement throughout this whole process has been both humbling and so welcomed. I love you all.

Thank you to those of you who joined the book waitlist. You sure know how to make a woman feel special. It was so helpful knowing you were there and being able to share my progress along the way. The emails I received from you meant the world to me, thank you. I hope the book is everything you hoped it would be.

To the generous women who took the time to review the book and give such beautiful feedback. I appreciate the preciousness of time and am so very grateful that you spent some of yours on my book.

To my darling husband, Chris. Your unwavering support has helped me take brave, bold steps that have led to experiences that have enriched my life in ways I never imagined. You've helped me see the strengths I've developed across my lifetime. You gently hold up my achievements when I minimise them and continue to bolster me when I want to shrink myself. Your steady presence has helped me move forward with clarity, purpose and intention. Your unfailing belief in me is so delightful, and I know I can shine brightly around you. Thanks for doing life with me, for your unconditional love, and for being such a wonderful dad to our darling son.

To my darling Matt, your pride in me warms my heart. I wouldn't be the woman I am today if I had not had the gift of you in my life. My most treasured role is being a mum, and I can't believe how lucky I am to be yours. You have brought immense joy into my life, and

## ACKNOWLEDGEMENTS

watching you grow into such a kind, generous, and compassionate man has been so heart-warming. You are so much wiser than I was at your age and I'm excited for what life holds for you. In many ways, you have been my greatest teacher and for that I thank you. I love you and the relationship we have so dearly, my darling.

I am grateful to my body for being persistent and loud when I wasn't listening. Living and learning through burnout and managing chronic illness has on reflection, been such a gift. It has led me to a new way of relating to myself and to restructuring my business and life in a way that is meaningful and sustainable.

This book has been written on Aboriginal Land. I acknowledge the First Nations people as Traditional Custodians of this land. I recognise their continuing connection to land, sea, culture and community. This land we now call Australia was never ceded. It always was and always will be Aboriginal land.

# *References*

Australian Institute of Family Studies. (2024). *Annual Report 2023–24*. Australian Government.

Australian Seniors. *Sandwich Generation Report 2025*. Australian Seniors Research Series. Published June 2025. Research conducted by MYMAVINS.

Breines, J. G., & Chen, S. (2012). Self-compassion increases self-improvement motivation. *Personality and Social Psychology Bulletin, 38*(9), 1133–1143. https://doi.org/10.1177/0146167212445599

Freudenberger, H. J. (1974). Staff burn-out. *Journal of Social Issues, 30*(1), 159–165. https://doi.org/10.1111/j.1540-4560.1974.tb00706.x

Gilbert, P. (2009). *The Compassionate Mind*. Little, Brown Book Group.

Gilbert, P., & Simos, G. (Eds.). (2022). *Compassion Focused Therapy: Clinical Practice and Applications*. Routledge.

Irons, C. & Beaumont, E. (2017). *The Compassionate Mind Workbook: A Step-by-Step Guide to Developing Your Compassionate Self*. Robinson.

Maslach, C. (1976). 'Burned-out', Human Behavior, 5(9), 16–22.

Matos, M., Duarte, J., Duarte, C., Gilbert, P., & Pinto-Gouveia, J. (2017). How one experiences and embodies compassionate mind training influences

## REFERENCES

its effectiveness. *Mindfulness, 9*(4), 1224–1235. https://doi.org/10.1007/s12671-017-0853-7

The CareSide. (2023). *Unpaid carers feel exhausted and invisible.* Australian Ageing Agenda. https://www.australianageingagenda.com.au/clinical/social-wellbeing/upaid-carers-feel-exhausted-and-invisible/

World Health Organization (2019). *Burnout an "occupational phenomenon": International Classification of Diseases*, 28 May 2019. Available at: https://www.who.int/news/item/28-05-2019-burn-out-an-occupational-phenomenon-international-classification-of-diseases European Parliament+15World Health Organization+15CWU union+15

# *About the author*

Dr Hayley D Quinn is a mindset and wellbeing coach, speaker, trainer, author and former clinical psychologist. She is the host of the *Welcome to Self®* podcast and past president of Compassionate Mind Australia. Hayley has extensive training in Compassion Focused Therapy; a framework she now uses in a non-clinical format and has trained professionals nationally and internationally.

Hayley is passionate about burnout prevention and helping women, non-binary and gender-diverse people transform their relationships with themselves and achieve their goals while prioritising sustainable practices, self-care, and compassion. She promotes a new model of sustainable success; one where personal wellbeing is no longer sacrificed. Hayley draws upon her personal experience of mental illness, domestic violence, solo parenting, business ownership, and burnout and recovery. She blends clinical expertise and science-backed approaches with real-world insights to empower people to transform how they work and live.

Hayley credits a compassionate relationship with herself as

fundamental in helping her recover from burnout and create a thriving life that honours her wellbeing. With a blend of empathy, compassion and practical skills, Hayley empowers her clients to embrace their authenticity, align with their values and build thriving lives and businesses that feel meaningful and purposeful.

Originally from the UK, Hayley lives on beautiful Gubbi Gubbi Country (Sunshine Coast), Australia, with her husband, Chris, and is mum to her adult son, Matt, whom she adores.

## *Where to from here*

Learn more about Dr Hayley's coaching and other services and access free resources and the *Welcome to Self®* podcast. These supports are here to help you take the next step in changing the relationship you have with yourself and creating the thriving life you dream about.

All services and resources are guided by an over-arching philosophy of compassion, with your wellbeing always at the heart.

🌐 drhayleydquinn.com ✉ hello@drhayleydquinn.com 📷 @drhayleydquinn

www.ingramcontent.com/pod-product-compliance
Lightning Source LLC
Chambersburg PA
CBHW031144020426
42333CB00013B/505